PATCHWORK ·USA

PATCHWORK USA

24 PROJECTS FOR YOUR HANDMADE JOURNEY

HEIDI STAPLES

Published in 2019
by Lucky Spool Media, LLC

www.luckyspool.com

5424 Sunol Blvd., Suite 10-118
Pleasanton, CA 94566
info@luckyspool.com

Text © Heidi Staples

Editor: Susanne Woods

Designer: Page + Pixel

Illustrator: Kari Vojtechovsky

Photographer: Page + Pixel

9 8 7 6 5 4 3 2 1

First Edition

Printed in China

Library of Congress Cataloging-in-
Publication Data available upon request

ISBN 978-1-940655-40-6

LSID0050

PATCHWORK USA

Key to Adventure

HISTORICAL MARKER
The story behind the project

SCENIC ROUTE
Design tips

ROTARY CLUB
Fabric and cutting requirements

TOUR GUIDE
Helpful hints

DETOUR
Project variations

They always say time changes things, but you actually have to change them yourself.

— Andy Warhol

$\mathcal{I}$NTRODUCTION

Is there anything that can put a smile on our faces like that beautiful word vacation? It brings to mind pictures of exotic destinations and long country roads. When life is busy, there's nothing so heavenly as taking time to relax.

The downside is that vacations are the exception . . . not the rule. Instead of jetting off to Hawaii tomorrow morning, I'll be washing dishes, grading papers, and doing laundry — important things, of course, but not quite the same as a tropical getaway. Life gets monotonous sometimes as we face the same daily whirlwind of responsibilities.

It's in those moments that I most need the creative outlet of patchwork. Those precious minutes at my sewing machine are more than just a hobby to me; they're my own little vacation from the stresses of life. Making the time to take a deep breath, set aside my chores, and sew something beautiful is a choice that refreshes my soul. I always seem to return to my work with a happier heart, ready to face the challenges of the day.

Whether you're vacationing at home or stitching your way across the country, I hope that you'll enjoy taking these sewing excursions along with me. After all, travel is always better with a friend.

Won't you join me?

CHAPTER ONE

Patchwork Begins at Home

ALL THINGS GREAT ARE WOUND
UP WITH ALL THINGS LITTLE.

— LUCY MAUD MONTGOMERY

Tools

Before we take off on this sewing journey together, let's talk about what you need for the ride. Getting ready to sew isn't all that different from getting ready for a trip. The more prepared you are, the more likely you're going to have a good time. If you have everything you need before you get started, you won't have to worry about hitting any speed bumps along the way. Patchwork requires only a few necessary tools, and there are also some specialty items that make the process easier if you have them. Let's take a look at what your packing list should include, whether you're sewing at home or away.

HAVE ON HAND...

① **SEWING MACHINE:** Buy the machine that fits what you plan to sew. Most people will do fine with a basic model, but upgrade if you can. I personally use a fairly inexpensive machine for all my sewing, my favorite features being the extension table and automatic thread cutter.

② **ROTARY CUTTER & EXTRA BLADES**

③ **RULERS:** It's worth having a variety of sizes on hand, including at least one long narrow ruler, one mid-size, and a few smaller ones for fussy cutting. My favorites are 3″ × 18″, 8½″ × 12½″, 6″ square, and 3½″ square.

④ **CUTTING MAT:** Buy the largest mat you can fit on your cutting table.

⑤ **SCISSORS:** I like to have one large pair for cutting yardage and a small pair for snipping threads and precision cutting.

⑥ **SEAM RIPPER**

⑦ **IRON**

⑧ **IRONING BOARD:** I use a homemade tabletop ironing board for 95% of my pressing, while my full size board is stored nearby for big jobs.

⑨ **PINS**

⑩ **HAND SEWING KIT:** learn more about this on page 29.

⑪ **THREAD:** Most of my machine sewing is done with off-white thread (Gutermann color #22) because I find it blends so well with different colors. I keep a rack full of colored Aurifil threads on hand, though, for special details.

⑫ **BINDING CLIPS:** I use these more often than pins when I sew. I find they work better at holding the pieces together for projects like bags, pillows, and pouches.

⑬ **FABRIC:** The bulk of my stash is quilting cotton, but I also keep varying amounts of linen, lawn, canvas, double gauze, flannel, knits and rayon in stock for different projects.

IT HELPS TO HAVE...

1. **ADHESIVE BASTING SPRAY:** I use this product constantly instead of basting pins when I'm making small projects. It holds everything together beautifully and doesn't leave any holes behind.

2. **GLUE PEN**

3. **TURNING TOOL:** I use a store-bought plastic tool that looks similar to a hera marker for most of my small projects, but sometimes a chopstick or knitting needle works better for larger items.

4. **THIMBLE:** I prefer a leather version to the traditional metal one, but what matters is that it comfortably fits your finger.

5. **DISAPPEARING INK FABRIC PEN**

6. **PINCUSHION OR PIN BOWL**

7. **SPRAY STARCH**

8. **SEAM ROLLER**

9. **QUILTING GLOVES:** Inexpensive garden gloves will work just as well, but use what's most comfortable.

10. **BASTING PINS:** I use these only when I'm basting a full-size quilt.

11. **PIECING LABELS:** these number or letter tags help you keep all the pieces straight so you don't forget what goes where.

Fabric Combinations

For me, there's nothing more important in a sewing project than the fabric I use to make it. The planning stage is my favorite, and it often takes the longest because I spend so much time choosing and arranging prints. Although there's nothing wrong with using a single fabric collection for a project, I love to use prints from a variety of collections and designers because I think an eclectic mix of fabrics gives each piece a more timeless look.

TRY SOME OF THESE TIPS AS YOU ARRANGE YOUR PRINTS

→ If you're putting things in color order, consider laying out the lines diagonally rather than up, down, or across.

→ Alternate colored shapes with low volume shapes to give the colors room to breathe.

→ Mix in solids or near solids along with prints so that the eye has a place to rest.

→ Be aware of the colors in your low volume prints. Try to place them where they will contrast or coordinate nicely with your colored prints to add more interest and variety to the mix. For example, place a low volume print with blue accents near a red or pink colored print.

Choosing fabrics is such a personal thing. Remember that there are no right or wrong answers here—just you and your stash working together to find the look that you want for this project. It really comes down to two things: how the fabrics make you feel and how they all work together. When I choose prints for my own work, I go through a checklist in my head that looks something like this:

ASK

DID I USE A GOOD MIX OF DESIGNS OR ARE THEY ALL THE SAME TYPE OF PRINT?
I LIKE TO INCLUDE AS MANY OPTIONS FROM THIS LIST AS POSSIBLE:

FLORAL flowers and other items from nature

GEOMETRIC shapes of all kinds

STRIPE lines in a row

DOT circles of any size

PLAID OR GINGHAM criss-crossing lines
and checkered squares

TEXT words or phrases

NOVELTY pictures and characters

SOLIDS one color only, no prints allowed

LOW VOLUME *(also known as high value)* designs on a white or light-colored background

LOW VALUE designs on a black or dark colored background

TONAL using only shades of the same color

SMALL SCALE tiny designs

LARGE SCALE big designs

DID I SPREAD THE COLORS OUT ACROSS THE PROJECT OR ARE THEY CLUSTERED TOGETHER?

DO THE COLORS COMPLEMENT EACH OTHER OR DO THEY CLASH?

DID I SPREAD OUT THE TYPES OF PRINTS ACROSS THE PROJECT OR DO I HAVE THE SAME KINDS OF DESIGNS RIGHT NEXT TO ONE ANOTHER (I.E. A TEXT PRINT BY ANOTHER TEXT PRINT)?

IS THIS MIX TOO BUSY? DO I NEED TO ADD MORE LOW VOLUME PRINTS, BASICS, OR SOLIDS TO CALM THINGS DOWN?

ARE THE PRINTS WORKING TOGETHER TO GIVE ME THE FEELING I WANT THIS PIECE TO CONVEY? IS IT HAPPY, SOFT, SWEET, BOLD, CHILDLIKE, QUIRKY, VINTAGE, MODERN, OR WHATEVER ELSE I AM TRYING TO SAY?

TRICKS FOR CHOOSING FABRICS

I KNOW THAT CHOOSING FABRICS CAN BE PARALYZING SOMETIMES, SO HERE ARE A FEW TRICKS TO GET YOU STARTED.

MORE IS MORE

This method works best in projects with lots of pieces, and the key is to get as much variety as you can in both the colors and the types of prints. The more fabrics you add, the more they will work together, so don't be afraid to be completely random in your choices.

KEEP TO A COLOR SCHEME

Even if your prints are completely different from each other, they will play together nicely if they stick to a specific range of colors. The tighter the range, the more curated your piece will look.

STICK TO A THEME

Travel, animals, books—pick a topic and choose fabrics to match. It's good to mix in some supporting basics to even things out, so don't feel like every piece has to obviously showcase the theme.

REMEMBER

It's your project and no one else's. If you want clashing colors and busy prints, then go for it. The key is knowing what you want before you get started so that you know how to get there. Like any road trip, you can't find your way on the map unless you know where you're going.

TINKER WITH YOUR FABRIC PULL

SOMETIMES YOU HAVE TO TINKER WITH A FABRIC PULL UNTIL YOU GET IT JUST THE WAY YOU WANT. HERE ARE SOME EXAMPLES OF HOW I WALK THROUGH THAT PROCESS.

HOW DO I PULL COLORS FROM ONE PRINT TO GUIDE MY COLOR SCHEME?

Choose your feature fabric first and make sure you bring a piece of it with you to actually hold up next to your fabric stash as you choose prints so that you get the shades right. Take note of at least 3 to 5 colors that you want to pull from the print. Start with a stack of 10-20 prints (depending on how large your project is) that might work and then narrow it down to the ones that fit the project or theme best. I liked that all these low volume prints had an illustrated look as well as an "outdoor garden" feel, which both went well with the hand drawn farmer mouse in the center. To bring some balance, I added a single light brown gingham which also fits the country theme and works as a quiet neutral between busier prints.

HOW DO I USE A LOT OF LOW VOLUME PRINTS WITHOUT THEM ALL BLENDING TOGETHER?

Pull colors from the low volume prints that will look good with all your fabrics, and then choose colored designs that you can alternate with the lighter ones. If you keep the colored prints simple, they will work almost like neutrals, letting the low volume prints stand out. This mix of prints was chosen with kids in mind, but has a more grown-up look due to the tight color scheme of pink, orange, white, gray and gold.

HOW DO I KEEP A SINGLE COLOR QUILT INTERESTING?

Remember that just because you're focusing on a single color doesn't mean that you can't use prints that include other colors too. As long as everything has the same background, multi-colored details will keep things interesting. To keep the project from being too uniform, try alternating your colored squares with low volume squares, here in shades of white and cream with only black designs on them. This is a trick that works beautifully with any color scheme, and you'll see it a lot in this book.

HOW DO I USE MORE VINTAGE COLORS LIKE BROWN IN A PROJECT WHILE STILL KEEPING IT MODERN?

This works best for me when the brown is either really dark or really light, giving it the neutrality of black or grey but with warmer overtones. For this mix, I pulled pink and orange shades from the brown dot print, adding in a light yellow to broaden the color range. I also featured a low volume print showing a slice of chocolate cake, giving me more brown and making a great focal point for the project. Another low volume text print with gold writing lightens things up even more.

HOW DO I WORK WITH TRICKY COMBINATIONS LIKE RED AND GREEN IN A PROJECT WITHOUT IT LOOKING TOO CHRISTMASSY?

The key is in the shades you use, the way you place them in the project, and the other colors you add to the mix. I used the low volume print to guide my color choices, going for strawberry shades with a healthy dose of blue. Mixing in several pink prints balances out the red as does adding both dark and light shades of blue. I try to also make sure that the only green I place next to my true red print is the lightest version of the color. As always, I'm careful with my placement, paying attention to where I put my novelty prints, text prints, and other design elements across the layout. I often imagine that I'm playing a game of Sudoku when it comes to placing colors and types of prints on a project, trying to have no more than one of each in every row across or down so that the piece will be nicely balanced.

HOW DO I KEEP A SET OF NOVELTY PRINTS FROM GETTING TOO BUSY?

Bring in your basics—and that doesn't mean that they have to be boring. This set of prints suggests that the project is for a child, so I went with a playful spin on primary colors. Rather than yellow, blue, and red, I chose supporting shades of gold, aqua, and a cross between purple and pink. The colors are all pulled from the prints I started with, so the fabrics play well together. Every design features simple backgrounds and patterns that are interesting to look at but still break up the clamor of the other fabrics. Remember too that once you sew your squares together, you'll be losing even more distractions in the seam allowances, helping the center of each print to really click into focus.

Visitor Center

Before we start the car, let's quickly review some basics. Are you an experienced sewist ready to choose your own road trip? Jump to page 34 to get started on my Daytrip projects. If you're a beginner, you can still easily tackle most of the projects in this book with nothing more than basic sewing skills. I've included a few helpful techniques in this section so that you can refer to them whenever you need a refresher. Be sure to check out the resource section in the back of this book for some wonderful websites and a list of other books that may be helpful for you as you begin. Here are a few of my favorite techniques that I use in making many of the projects in this book.

FUSSY CUTTING

There are times when I want to just cut random pieces of fabric for my projects, but not usually. Much of my work features fussy cutting, which is nothing more than positioning your ruler carefully as you cut to show off a certain part of the fabric. I love that this process helps me turn the spotlight on details in a print that might otherwise go unnoticed. The three simplest methods for fussy cutting are:

1 Have a variety of small cutting rulers on hand for the sizes you fussy cut most often.

2 Use washi tape to mark off the size you want on a larger ruler.

3 Get in the habit of eyeballing it. If you need a 2½″ square, position the center of that square on your ruler (1¼″ from both sides) over the center of the design you want to fussy cut and trim accordingly. I use this method more than any other, and the more you practice, the easier it is to do.

I keep a Fussy Cut Box on my cutting table, which is just a small wooden box divided into compartments. When I'm prepping fabric for a project, I will often fussy cut a few extra squares and sort them into the box by size. It's a lifesaver when I need to sew a patchwork project in a hurry!

NESTING SEAMS

The easiest way to get your seams to match up perfectly in a project is to nest them. Taking an extra minute to follow these steps will make your patchwork look amazing every time.

1 Press your seams in opposite directions, preferably towards the darker fabric if you can.

2 Place the two blocks right sides together, matching up the seams. You'll feel a little bump where the seam has been pressed down on each block. Gently pull them together until those two bumps nest right up against each other.

3 Use pins or binding clips either directly on the seam or just above and below the seam to hold the pieces together and then sew.

HALF-SQUARE TRIANGLES

Rather than cutting out triangles and sewing them together individually, take a shortcut by using this quick method for turning out tidy half-square triangles in pairs.

1 Fold one of your two squares in half diagonally with wrong sides together and press gently or use a marking pen and ruler to create a line.

2 Place two squares with right sides together and stitch ¼" on either side of the pressed or marked line from Step 1. Use a rotary cutter to trim along that line.

3 Press each of the half-square triangles open and trim to the correct size for your project, making sure that the diagonal line of your final square size matches up with the diagonal seam across the square.

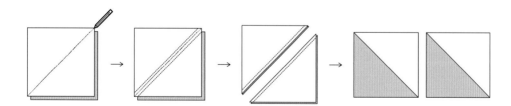

A HAND-SEWING BASICS KIT

I do most of my quilting by machine, but sometimes I like to quilt by hand. I love that it makes a project even more personal, both in the making and giving of the piece. There are wonderful tutorials online that will give you details on hand sewing, but if you want to dive right in, here are the basic tools you'll need in your kit:

1 NEEDLES I always use appliqué sharps because I love the way they glide easily through fabric.

2 THIMBLE I prefer a leather version to the traditional metal one, but what matters is that it comfortably fits your finger. Try out a few to find your perfect fit.

3 THREAD I typically use Aurifloss for my hand quilting, though I occasionally use standard thread if I want a lighter line of stitches.

4 EMBROIDERY SCISSORS A sharp pair of snips is a must. I use these all the time, even with my machine sewing.

5 HERA MARKER AND RULER I don't like using even disappearing ink pens on my projects unless I have to. These tools are great for marking temporary lines for quilting.

BASTING AND SEWING HEXAGONS

Sewing together hexagons by hand can seem intimidating, but it's actually easy to pick up. Best of all, hexagons make any project look impressive.

BASTING HEXAGONS

1 Place a paper hexagon template in the center of the wrong side of your fabric square or hexagon. You can photocopy this template or use specially made paper pieces.

2 Fold the fabric back over one edge of your template (Fig. 1) and, holding it down with your finger, fold the fabric back over the next edge to the left of it. Using your needle and thread, stitch from right to left through the fold of the fabric without stitching through the template.

Figure 1   Figure 2

3 Continue folding the fabric back over each successive edge of the template until you come back to where you started. Make a final stitch to hold everything in place and cut your thread, leaving a short tail (Fig. 2). Press gently.

SEWING HEXAGONS

1 Place two basted hexagons right sides together, aligning one edge. Starting from the right, make 2-3 stitches through the top corner to secure your thread and then whipstitch across the edge. Make 2-3 stitches through the top left corner to finish and then trim the thread (Fig. 3). Repeat until you have a row of hexagons.

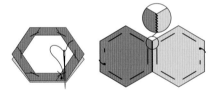

Figure 3

2 Repeat Step 1 until all the rows for your project are finished.

3 To sew the rows together, follow the same procedure as in Step 1, this time starting from the end of each row. Carefully position the rows so that the edges align correctly each time you need to sew them together. Once you have sewn all the rows together in pairs, sew the pairs

together until you have a finished hexagon panel. (Fig. 4)

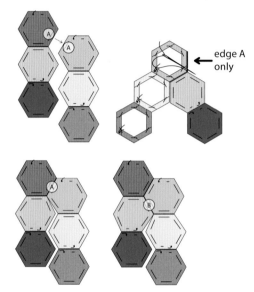

edge A only

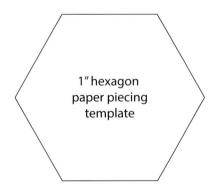

Figure 4

1" hexagon paper piecing template

FINISHING A ZIPPER POUCH

Few things strike fear in the creative heart as much as your first attempt to make a zipper pouch. Follow these steps carefully and you'll be a pro in no time.

1 Stack from bottom to the top in this order along the upper edge of each piece: front exterior piece (right side up), zipper (right side down) and the lining piece (wrong side up). Stitch ¼″ from the edge. (Fig. 1)

2 Press the lining piece back from the zipper (don't press back the front exterior yet) and topstitch the lining in place against the zipper ⅛″ from the edge. Now press the front exterior back from the zipper also.

3 Repeat Steps 1-2 on the opposite side of the zipper with the back exterior piece and remaining lining piece.

4 Unzip the zipper at least halfway and fold the exterior pieces away from the zipper so that they lie on top of each other, right sides of the fabric together and the zipper pointed in their direction. Clip or pin them together. Then clip or pin the lining pieces (again right sides together) on the other side of the zipper.

5 Starting on the long edge of the lining pieces, sew ¼″ from the edge all the way around the pouch pieces, leaving a 2″ to 6″ gap (depending on the size of the project) in the bottom of the lining and backstitching at the start and finish. (Fig. 2)

6 Trim off the excess zipper. Pull the exterior right side out through the gap in the lining, push out the corners with a turning tool, and press. Tuck the raw edges inside the gap, press, and sew ⅛″-¹⁄₁₆″ from the edge to sew the opening closed. Push the lining inside the pouch and press.

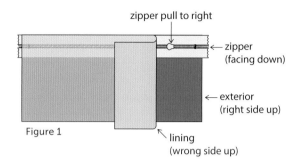

zipper pull to right

zipper (facing down)

exterior (right side up)

Figure 1

lining (wrong side up)

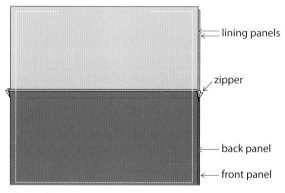

lining panels

zipper

back panel

front panel

Figure 2

SNOWBALLING A CORNER

This technique gets its name from a snowball quilt block, which is created by this easy but extremely useful process.

1 Divide the background squares in half diagonally either by drawing a line with a pencil or by folding the square in half diagonally and pressing to create a crease.

2 Place the background square in one corner of the feature square with the right sides together, making sure the diagonal line cuts across the corner correctly.

3 Stitch on the diagonal line, trim the seam to ¼", and press open. Repeat for all four corners.

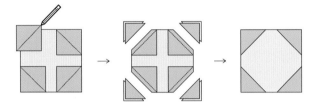

MAKING STRAPS OR HANDLES

This is actually just quilt binding that's been sewn together with the long edges folded inside. We'll use it for two projects later, but you can follow these directions to add a strap to any pouch or bag in this book.

1 Fold the fabric strip in half lengthwise and press.

2 Unfold. Then fold the long sides in to meet at the center. Press again.

3 Open and refold on the center fold, enclosing the raw ends inside. Edgestitch along both long sides to finish.

Reading the Map

The project chapters in this book are divided into three sections: Daytrips (simple projects), Weekend Getaways (slightly more complex projects), and Summer Vacation (projects that will take a bit longer). These categories aren't set in stone. Depending on your skill level and schedule, you may find that some of these pieces take you more or less time to finish, but this should give you a rough idea of how long things should take and help you pick the right pattern when you need it.

There are some guidelines and abbreviations that will be true for all projects, so rather than writing them in the directions each time, here they are:

→ Press all fabrics well before cutting.

→ Seam allowances are ¼˝ unless otherwise noted.

→ Press seams open or towards the darker fabric unless otherwise instructed.

→ RST = right sides together (right side being the printed side)

→ WST = wrong sides together

→ WOF = width of fabric

→ HST = half-square triangle

CHAPTER TWO

DAYTRIPS

Ah, Daytrips! Growing up in Southern California, I lived about an hour away from all sorts of attractions. Every Friday after my sister and I finished our homeschool classes for the week, we enjoyed a day of family fun: cookouts at the beach, visits to the local craft fair and trips to Disneyland. There was something wonderful about being able to jump into the car and head off for an adventure not too far from home.

Is there anything more fun than sewing daytrips, those lovely projects that we can start and finish before the day is done? Granted, some of us have more time in a day to sew than others, but these projects should take you no more than a weekend to finish unless you have some serious distractions going on at your house. When you need a last minute gift, a fast finish, or just a creative break from a bigger project, this is the chapter for you.

MAY YOU LIVE ALL THE DAYS
OF YOUR LIFE.
— Jonathan Swift

Tagalong Pincushion

HISTORICAL MARKER

This tiny pincushion is the perfect tagalong when you're sewing. It's a great scrap buster and they make sweet little gifts for friends. Once you start making them, it's hard to stop!

SCENIC ROUTE

I like to pick my center fabric first and use that as a guide for the rest of my choices. The other fabrics can either coordinate with the theme or follow the same color scheme. Linen makes a soft, sturdy backing for the cushion itself.

FINISHED SIZE: 3˝ square

1 Referencing Figure 1, arrange and sew the cut units from Fabrics A, B and C into a 3 × 3 grid.

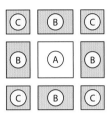

Figure 1

2 Sew the shorter background rectangles to the right and left edges of the assembled unit from Step 1 and press. Sew the longer background rectangles to the upper and lower edges and press again.

3 Following the manufacturer's instructions, spray one side of the batting with adhesive basting spray and layer the assembled unit from Step 2 right side up. Quilt as desired.

4 Fold the twill tape in half with the WST. Center the tape along one edge on the right side of the pincushion front, aligning the raw edges. Baste in place using a ⅛˝ seam allowance. (Fig. 2)

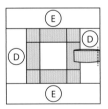

Figure 2

5 Position the assembled unit from Step 4 and the backing square RST. Sew around the pincushion, leaving a 2˝ gap in one side for turning.

6 Turn right side out through the opening from Step 5 and gently push out the corners with turning tool or similar blunt object.

7 Fill with stuffing (and add in the weights if using), then hand stitch the opening closed. Hand sew the button onto the twill tape.

✴ ROTARY CLUB

From Fabric A, fussy cut (see page 27):
(1) 1½˝ square

From a 5˝ square of Fabric B, cut:
(4) 1˝ × 1½˝ rectangles

From a 5˝ square (or larger depending on the repeat of the motif desired) of Fabric C, fussy cut:
(4) 1˝ squares

From a 10˝ square of Background Fabric, cut:
(2) 1˝ × 3½˝ rectangles (D)
(2) 1˝ × 2½˝ rectangles (E)

From the Batting and Background Fabric, cut:
(1) 3½˝ square

ADDITIONAL SUPPLIES

- 5oz of polyfill for stuffing
- (1) 2¼˝ length of ⅝˝ wide twill tape
- (1) 1˝ button
- Adhesive basting spray
- Hand sewing basics kit (see page 29)
- *Optional:* Weights

Postcard Kit

HISTORICAL MARKER

My daughters are crazy about postcards, and whenever we travel, they always pick up a few to send home to family while we're away. This kit is a great place to keep your own stationery—note cards, postcards, or whatever you like to share with your loved ones.

SCENIC ROUTE

Text prints of any kind work on the message side of the postcard. Fussy cutting comes in different sizes for this project—a small scrap for the stamp and large piece for the feature side of the card. Map prints are always a fun choice for the picture.

FINISHED SIZE: 5⅛″ × 7″ closed

① Referencing Figures 1 and 2, arrange the Exterior fabrics on a flat surface. Sew the B strips to the short ends of the A rectangle and press. Sew the C strip to the outer long edge and the wider D strip to the other long edge (this will be the middle of the kit).

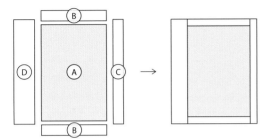

Figure 1

② Referencing Figure 2, sew the E strip to one long edge of the J rectangle and an H strip to the opposite long edge. Press.

③ Sew the F and L rectangles together along their 1½″ edge and press. Sew the G rectangle along the right edge, then the K rectangle to the opposite long edge of the G rectangle and press. Sew the remaining H rectangle to the top long edge of the assembled unit and press.

④ Sew the assembled unit from Step 2 to the assembled unit from Step 3. Press. Sew the remaining C strip to the left long edge, nearest the stamp L rectangle.

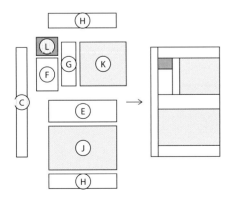

Figure 2

ROTARY CLUB

From the Postcard Fabric, cut:

(1) 5″ × 7″ rectangle (A)

From a fat quarter of Background Fabric, cut:

(2) ¾″ × 5″ strips (B)

(2) ¾″ × 7½″ strips (C)

(1) 1½″ × 7½″ strip (D)

(1) 1½″ × 4¾″ rectangle (E)

(1) 1½″ × 2¼″ rectangle (F)

(1) 1″ × 3″ rectangle (G)

(2) 1″ × 4¾″ rectangles (H)

(1) 7½″ × 10¾″ rectangle (I)

From a 10″ square of Text Print, cut:

(1) 3″ × 4¾″ rectangle (J)

(1) 3″ × 3¼″ rectangle (K)

From a scrap of Lavender Fabric, cut:

(1) 1¼″ × 1½″ rectangle for the stamp (L)

From a 10″ square of Muslin, cut:

(2) 4¼″ × 7½″ rectangles (M)

From a fat quarter of Pink Fabric, cut:

(2) 7½″ × 8½″ rectangles (N)

From the Batting, cut:

(1) 7½″ × 10¾″ rectangle

ADDITIONAL SUPPLIES

- (2) 4″ × 7″ rectangles of heavyweight sew-in interfacing
- (1) 1¾″ length of ⅝″ wide twill tape (O)
- Adhesive basting spray
- Binding clips
- Hair elastic
- Hand sewing basics kit (see page 29)
- (1) ¾″ button

5 Sew the assembled unit from Step 4 to the assembled unit from Step 1 and press. Following the manufacturer's instructions, apply adhesive basting spray to the wrong side of the Exterior panel and layer the rectangle of batting to fuse them together. Quilt as desired.

6 Fold the twill tape in half with the WST. Position the tape along the B strip, 1½˝ away from the lower right corner. Align the raw edges and baste in place using a ⅛˝ seam allowance. (Fig. 3)

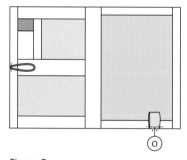

Figure 3

7 To complete the Exterior assembly, cut the hair elastic being sure to remove any metal hardware, and fold it in half. Center the raw ends on the C strip (Fig. 3). Align the raw edges and baste in place.

8 Fold an N rectangle in half with the WST so that short raw edges meet and press. Slip a rectangle of M muslin interfacing between the layers making sure the long edge is snugly against the fold. Edgestitch through all of the layers along the right side of the fold. Repeat for the second N rectangle and M interfacing rectangle to create the Pockets.

9 Referencing Figure 4, align the short end of each assembled Pocket from Step 8 with the short sides of the I rectangle. Finish the Lining assembly by basting the Pockets in place, sewing through all of the layers.

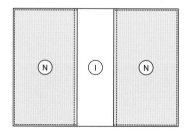

Figure 4

10 Place the Lining and Exterior panels RST and secure in place using binding clips. Be sure that the twill tape and elastic are nested between the layers.

Sew ¼˝ from the edge around the rectangle, leaving a 6˝ gap in the center of one long side for turning. Clip the corners to reduce the bulk, then turn the assembled unit right side out. Gently push out the corners with a turning tool.

11 Slip a rectangle of the heavyweight interfacing inside the gap, positioning one in the center of each half of the kit. Tuck the raw edges of the opening from Step 10 inside and give the entire kit a good press. Edgestitch around the perimeter and then stitch a line down the center of the kit across the D strip.

12 Fold the assembled kit in half and bring the elastic loop around to the right side of rectangle A. Mark a point approximately ½˝ away from the edge of rectangle C on the A rectangle. Hand sew the button in place at the mark, being careful not to sew the pocket shut.

ROAD TRIP PILLOW

HISTORICAL MARKER

I've found that one of the most useful gifts I can make for friends is a small rectangular pillow. Travelers enjoy the extra cushion on road trips. New moms use it as an arm rest during feedings. Patients recovering from surgery tell me how comforting it is to have in a hospital bed. Easily sewn together in an afternoon, it makes a wonderful last-minute gift.

SCENIC ROUTE

I like to use diagonal bands of color in rainbow order alternating with neutrals. Try sprinkling a few low-volume prints in with the background solids to give the pillow lots of interest. For this version, I used my stash of linen and canvas, but you could use quilting cottons or lawn instead. This project is a great introduction to fussy cutting, so pull out your favorite novelty prints!

FINISHED SIZE: 12" x 16"

① Referencing the Assembly Diagram, arrange the A squares into a 6 × 8 grid.

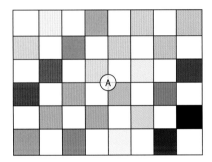

Assembly Diagram

② Sew the squares together in pairs, then sew the pairs together into quartets. Sew the quartets together into vertical rows, alternating pressing up or down for each row. Finally sew all 4 vertical rows together. Press the assembled Exterior well.

③ Following the manufacturer's instructions, apply adhesive basting spray to the wrong side of the Exterior panel. Layer the Batting rectangle and apply another layer of adhesive to the Batting itself. Layer the lining rectangle over the Batting with the right side up. Quilt as desired. Trim away any excess Batting and Lining to 12½″ × 16½″ rectangle.

④ With the wrong sides facing, fold a 12½″ edge of the Backing rectangle in by ½″ towards the wrong side of the fabric. Press. Make a second ½″ fold, enclosing the raw edges. Topstitch ¼″ from the outer folded edge (Fig. 1). Repeat with the second Backing rectangle.

Figure 1

ROTARY CLUB

From a selection of Colored Scraps, cut:

    (24) 2½″ squares (A)

From a selection of Off-White Fabrics, cut:

    (24) 2½″ squares (A)

From a fat quarter of Backing Fabric, cut:

    (2) 11″ × 12½″ rectangles (B)

From the Batting and Lining Fabric, cut:

    (1) 14″ × 18″ rectangle

ADDITIONAL SUPPLIES

- Adhesive basting spray
- Binding clips
- Turning tool
- 12″ × 16″ pillow form

5 With the patchwork Exterior from Step 3 facing right side up, layer one assembled Backing from Step 4, right side down, aligning the short raw edges. Layer the remaining Backing rectangle aligning the short raw edges on the opposite side. The topstitched folds of the Backing should overlap. Use the binding clips to hold the layers in place and sew around the perimeter (Fig. 2). Trim the corners to reduce the bulk.

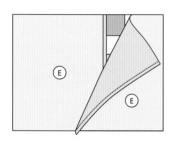

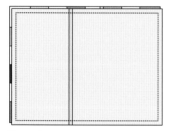

Figure 2

 TOUR GUIDE

When sewing pillow pieces together in Step 5, stitch at least twice over the long sides where the hemmed Backing edges are attached. This will keep your cover from ripping apart when you insert the pillow form.

6 Using a turning tool or similar blunt object, carefully push out the corners. Press well and insert the 12″ × 16″ pillow form.

DETOUR

Adjust this pattern by measuring the width and length of the pillow you want to cover, dividing those numbers by 2, and then multiplying them together to get the number of 2½″ squares you'll need. For instance, a 16″ × 16″ pillow would be 8 × 8 = 64. Arrange your 64 squares in a grid of 8 × 8, sew them together, and you'll have a pillow top that will fit!

SNAPSHOT NEEDLEBOOK

HISTORICAL MARKER

This needlebook is a nod to my love of vintage photos. Whether they involve family members or total strangers, I'm always fascinated by looking into the eyes of people from the past. This project makes a wonderful extra treat to tuck in with sewing swaps, but I personally just enjoy sewing them up and adding them to the growing miniature library on a shelf in my sewing room.

SCENIC ROUTE

The fussy cut "photo" on the cover of this book is a great way to feature one of your favorite prints. I use a solid or textured white print for the edging and black solid for the photo corners, as it really does give the appearance of a picture in an old album.

FINISHED SIZE: 4″ × 4″ × ½″ closed

① Sew a short Fabric B rectangle to the opposite edges of the A square and press. Sew a longer Fabric B strip to the remaining sides of the A square and press again.

② Use the Fabric C squares to snowball all four corners of the panel following the instructions on page 32. (Fig. 1)

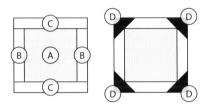

Figure 1

③ Referencing Figure 2, sew the short Background rectangles to the top and bottom edges of the assembled unit from Step 2 and press. Sew the narrower rectangle to the right edge and the larger Background rectangle to left edge. Press.

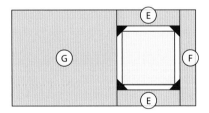

Figure 2

④ Following the manufacturer's instructions, apply basting spray to the wrong side of the assembled unit from Step 3 and layer the Batting to fuse it in place. Quilt as desired. Trim away any excess Batting so that the completed Exterior panel measures 4½″ × 8¾″.

 ROTARY CLUB

From a scrap of Focal Fabric, fussy cut (see page 27):

(1) 3″ square (A)

From a 10″ square of Border Fabric, cut:

(2) ¾″ × 3″ rectangles (B)

(2) ¾″ × 3½″ rectangles (C)

From a 5″ square of Black Fabric, cut:

(4) 1″ squares (D)

From a fat quarter of Background Fabric, cut:

(2) 1″ × 3½″ rectangles (E)

(1) 1″ × 4½″ rectangle (F)

(1) 4½″ × 5¼″ rectangle (G)

From the Batting, cut:

(1) 5″ × 9½″ rectangle (H)

From a 10″ square of Lining Fabric, cut:

(2) 4½″ × 4⅝″ rectangles (I)

From a 10″ square of Felt, cut:

(2) 3½″ × 3¾″ rectangles (J)

ADDITIONAL SUPPLIES

- Adhesive basting spray
- Binding clips
- Turning tool

5 With the right side facing up, layer the two Felt rectangles centered on a Lining rectangle with the short raw edges on one side aligned. Position the remaining Lining rectangle on top with the wrong side facing up and aligning all of the raw edges with the other Lining rectangle. (Fig. 3)

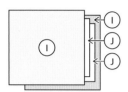

Figure 3

6 Sew along the edge of the stack where all four edges are aligned, being sure to go through all of the layers. (Fig. 4)

Figure 4

7 Open the assembled Lining panel from Step 5 so that it lies flat with all of the Felt pages to one side. Place the Exterior panel on top of the Lining, RST, and clip or pin them together.

8 Sew around the perimeter, leaving a 3″ gap along one side for turning and backstitching at the start and finish of the line of stitching. Trim the corners to reduce the bulk and turn the book right side out through the gap.

9 Using a turning tool or similar blunt object, gently push out the corners. Tuck the raw edges inside the gap and press. Edgestitch around the perimeter, closing the gap in the process. Close the book and press.

 TOUR GUIDE

Both times you approach the book's "spine" (halfway along the long side of the book) when edgestitching in Step 9, keep the needle down in the fabric, lift up the presser foot, and carefully flip the felt pages under the book so that the raw edges are facing away from you and behind the needle before you continue stitching. This will make it easier to get a neat line of stitching around the entire book.

COFFEE SHOP COASTERS

HISTORICAL MARKER

I love roadside diners and coffee shops. There's nothing like those vinyl booths in pastel colors, the glass covered cakes and pies on the counter, and the classic tunes playing on the jukebox. It's all retro heaven, inspiring me to bring a bit of that candy-colored nostalgia home with us. With seven people in our house, coffee mugs and milk glasses seem to multiply overnight. Having a stack of coasters on hand is a must to save our wooden side tables from a tragic end. Sew up a handful of these color coordinated beauties in under an hour, and believe me, your furniture will thank you.

SCENIC ROUTE

Each coaster features different shades of the same color. I like the contrast of using solids for the cross and a coordinating low volume print for the background. You can fussy cut these if you like, but they work just as well if you don't. These directions will give you one coaster, so multiply to make as many as you like!

FINISHED SIZE:
5˝ square, Makes 1 Coaster

1 Referencing the Assembly Diagram, arrange Fabrics A-C in a 3 x 3 grid. Sew the units together into three rows. Press the seams in the middle row in the opposite direction from the other two so that the seams nest (see page 27). Sew the three rows together.

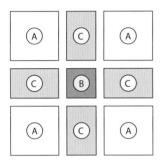

Assembly Diagram

2 Following the manufacturer's instructions, apply the basting spray to the wrong side of the assembled unit from Step 1, and layer the Batting on top. Quilt as desired.

3 Place the quilted unit from Step 2 and the Backing square RST. Sew around the perimeter of the square, leaving a 3˝ gap on one side for turning and being sure to backstitch at the start and finish of the seam. Clip the corners to reduce the bulk.

4 Turn the coaster right side out through the gap from Step 3, gently pushing out the corners with a turning tool or similar blunt object. Tuck the raw edges inside the gap and press. Edgestitch to finish.

ROTARY CLUB

From a 10˝ square of Fabric A, cut:
(4) 2½˝ squares

From a scrap of Fabric B, cut:
(1) 1½˝ square

From a 10˝ square of Fabric C, cut:
(4) 1½˝ × 2½˝ rectangles

From the Backing Fabric, cut:
(1) 5½˝ square

From the Batting, cut:
(1) 5½˝ square

ADDITIONAL SUPPLIES

- Adhesive basting spray
- Turning tool

BOARDWALK MINI TOTE

HISTORICAL MARKER

Who doesn't love a day at the beach? Save that giant tote for when you and the family are ready for an afternoon of building sand castles and jumping in the waves. When you're taking a stroll on the pier or going window shopping on the boardwalk, this miniature version of the classic oversized beach bag is all that you need. If I can carry this mini tote packed with just the essentials in one hand and an ice cream cone in the other, I'm a very happy woman.

SCENIC ROUTE

I chose a limited color spectrum for the patchwork panels which look great paired with the texture of a linen accent to complete the Exterior. The unusual addition of rope handles adds to the beachy feel of this bag and are easy to attach.

FINISHED SIZE:
8½" wide x 8¼" high x 3½" deep

① Sew the Colored strips together along their long sides. Press gently, being sure not to distort the rectangular shape of the panel. Cut in half along the long side, trimming each half to 8″ tall × 12½″ wide.

② With the RST, sew an Accent rectangle to the long edge of Patchwork panel from Step 1 and press. Repeat. Following the manufacturer's instructions, apply the basting spray to the wrong side of the Exterior and center on top of the Batting. On the right side of the assembled unit, topstitch (by hand or machine) on the Accent rectangle, approximately ¼″ below the seam.

③ Referencing the Assembly Diagram, position the cut ends of the cording or rope at the seam between the second and third strips in from each side. Be sure the raw edges are aligned and baste them in place using a ⅛″ seam allowance. Repeat with the other piece of cording or rope on the second assembled Exterior panel.

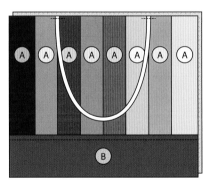

Assembly Diagram

ROTARY CLUB

From a selection of 8 Colored Fabrics, cut:

(1) 2″ × 16″ strip from each (A)

From a fat quarter of Accent Fabric, cut:

(2) 12½″ × 3″ rectangles (B)

From ⅓ of a yard of Lining Fabric, cut:

(2) 10½″ × 12½″ rectangles

From a half yard of the Batting, cut:

(4) 10½″ × 12½″ rectangles

ADDITIONAL SUPPLIES

- (2) 15″ lengths of ¼″ thick cording or rope
- Adhesive basting spray
- Turning tool
- Marking tool
- Binding clips
- Hand sewing kit (see page 29)

④ With the two Exterior panels RST, and being sure the seam which joins the Patchwork panel to the Accent rectangle is aligned on both sides. Secure the layers together using binding clips. Sew around the sides and lower edge of the panels, backstitching at the start and finish. Carefully cut a 2″ square from each lower corner. (Fig. 1)

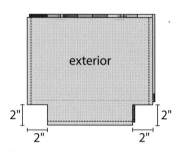

Figure 1

⑤ Pinch and nest the side and lower seams, aligning the raw edges. Stitch along the raw edge at least twice for extra strength (Fig. 2). Repeat with the opposite corner. Turn the bag right side out.

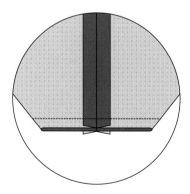

Figure 2

⑥ Using the basting spray, attach the remaining Batting rectangles to the wrong side of the Lining rectangles. Repeat Step 4, but leave a 6″ gap in the base seam for turning.

⑦ Repeat Step 5, but leave the Lining wrong side out.

⑧ Slip the bag Exterior inside the bag Lining with the RST, checking that the side seams and top raw edges align and that the handles are sandwiched between the layers of fabric (Fig. 3). Use binding clips to hold both pieces together at the top and then stitch around the circumference.

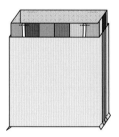

Figure 3

⑨ Pull the bag Exterior through hole in the Lining, pushing out the corners of the bag and pressing carefully. Tuck the raw edges inside the opening in Lining with the WST. Press and hand or machine stitch the gap closed. Gently push the Lining down into the bag.

⑩ Edgestitch around the top of the bag to finish.

PENNY POUCH

HISTORICAL MARKER

Confession: I adore tiny scraps but don't have the patience to spend weeks making quilts from them. This little pouch saves the day, giving me the chance to use my favorite pieces in a project that takes no more than a day to sew. Patchwork to the rescue again!

SCENIC ROUTE

Pink takes a patriotic red, white, and blue color scheme up a notch, giving this pouch an airy, almost old-fashioned look. Neutral linen keeps things light and adds a bit of texture.

FINISHED SIZE: 5˝ square

1 Referencing the Assembly Diagram, arrange one set of 15 A squares into a 3 × 5 grid. Sew the squares into three rows. Press the seams in the middle row to the opposite side of the other two. Nest the seams for each row (see page 27) and sew the rows together.

2 With the RST, sew a B rectangle to a long side of the Patchwork panel. Press the seams open. Following the manufacturer's instructions, apply basting spray to the wrong side of the assembled Exterior. Layer the Batting square, aligning the raw edges. Quilt as desired on the Patchwork panel only.

3 Topstitch ⅛˝ away from the seam on each side of the Exterior.

4 Repeat Steps 1-3 with the remaining set of A and B pieces.

5 On the right side of an Exterior panel, use the template provided (see page 127) to trace a curve on the B rectangle. Cut along the drawn line. Repeat for the second Exterior panel and two Lining panels.

6 Fold the twill tape in half with the WST. Using a ⅛˝ seam allowance, baste in place just above the seam between the top and middle row of the patchwork squares on the right side of an Exterior panel. If desired, hand sew three buttons along the seam between the Patchwork and B rectangle. Ensure that the button closest to the raw edge will not interfere with the seam allowance.

7 Finish the pouch according to the instructions on page 31.

8 Thread the leather lacing through the zipper. Knot. Trim the ends at matching angles.

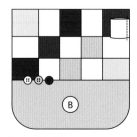

Assembly Diagram

ROTARY CLUB

From a selection of 15 Colored Fabrics, in shades of pink, red, white, light blue and navy, cut:

(2) 1½˝ squares from each print (A)

From a 10˝ square of Linen Fabric, cut:

(2) 5½˝ × 2½˝ rectangles for the exterior accent (B)

From an 11˝ square of Pink Fabric, cut:

(2) 5½˝ squares for the Lining

From the Batting, cut:

(2) 5½˝ squares

ADDITIONAL SUPPLIES

- Adhesive basting spray
- Template on page 127
- Marking tool
- (1) 1½˝ length of ⅝˝ wide twill tape
- (3) ⅜˝ buttons
- (1) 7˝ zipper
- (1) 7˝ length of ⅛˝ wide leather lacing
- Hand sewing kit (see page 29)

KITCHENETTE SET

HISTORICAL MARKER

Sometimes you have to make your own fun, and what better way to do it than with a cute sewing project? During the winter doldrums one year, I tried to liven things up at our house by having an afternoon tea party with my daughters every Friday to celebrate the end of another school week. I came up with the idea of these placemats to make our parties festive, but my girls mostly love using them for breakfast in the mornings as a cheerful way to start the day. Try using them for a cute traveling snack mat too.

SCENIC ROUTE

I love making each mat with fabrics in a different color for a patchwork rainbow across my table, and alternating low volume and colored rectangles gives them a nice balance. Try to mix in some fussy cut pieces which are fun for kids to look at while they're eating. The directions below will give you one mat, so multiply as needed.

FINISHED SIZE:
10½˝ x 10˝, Makes 1 Mat

① Referencing the Assembly Diagram, arrange the focus color rectangles and the background rectangles into a 3 × 4 grid. Sew the rectangles into four rows of three rectangles each. Press the seams in each row to opposites sides. Nest the seams for each row and sew the rows together.

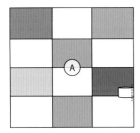

Assembly Diagram

② Following the manufacturer's instructions, apply basting spray to the wrong side of the assembled unit from Step 1 and center the Batting on top. Quilt as desired.

③ Fold the twill tape in half with WST. Position the tape just above the lowest seam on the right side of the Exterior, aligning the raw edges. Baste in place using a ⅛" seam allowance.

④ With the Exterior and Backing rectangle RST, secure the layers using binding clips. Be sure that the twill tape is nested between the layers. Sew around the perimeter, leaving a 3-4" gap on one side for turning and back stitching at the start and finish of the line of sewing. Trim the corners to reduce the bulk.

⑤ Turn the mat right side out through the gap from Step 3. Use a turning tool to gently push out the corners. Tuck the raw edges inside the gap, press and edgestitch around the perimeter, closing the gap in the process.

ROTARY CLUB

From a selection of 6 Focus Color Fabrics, cut:

(1) 3″ × 4″ rectangle from each

From a fat quarter of Background Fabric, cut:

(6) 3″ × 4″ rectangles

From the Lining and Batting, cut:

(1) 11″ × 10½″ rectangle from each

ADDITIONAL SUPPLIES

- (1) 1¾″ length of ⅝″ wide twill tape
- Adhesive basting spray
- Turning tool
- Binding clips
- Hand sewing kit (see page 29)

CHAPTER THREE

WEEKEND GETAWAYS

I'll never forget the time my husband surprised me with a weekend in San Diego. I was worn out from a new job and still adjusting to the demands of young motherhood. He told me to pack a bag, left our baby with my parents, and whisked me away to a beautiful inn for 2 days of fun and relaxation. I've always tucked that weekend away in my heart as one of the sweetest things he has ever done for me.

Weekend getaways are a beautiful pause in the middle of a busy life, and I hope that you'll find the projects in this chapter to be just as refreshing. These items might take you more than a day to finish, but they're still relatively short-term commitments, making them great choices for a weekend retreat or Saturday sew-in. Best of all, many are wonderful travel accessories if you want to take a trip of your own!

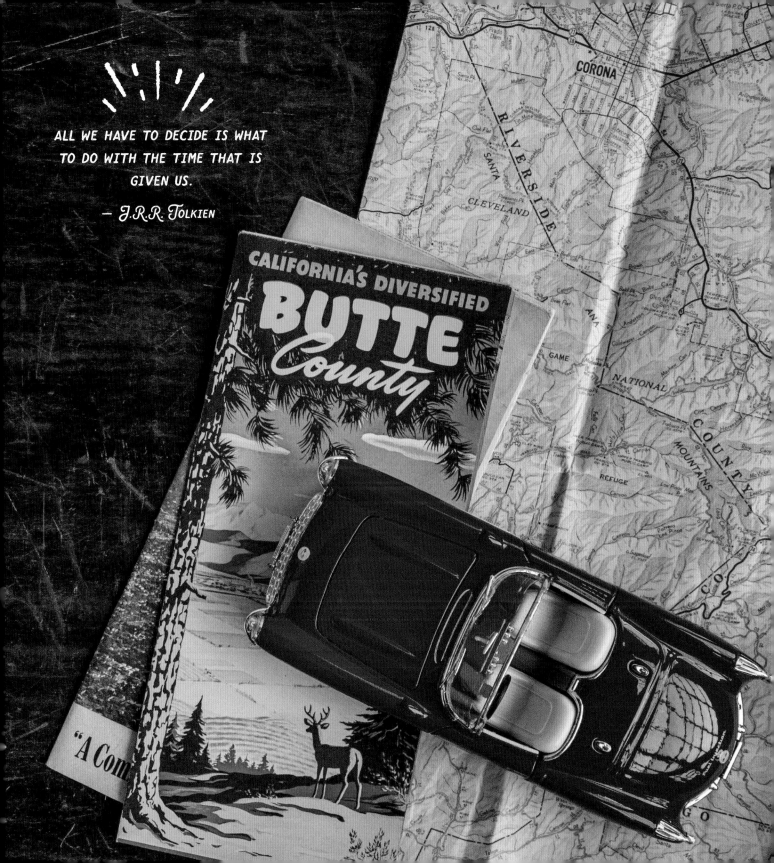

ALL WE HAVE TO DECIDE IS WHAT
TO DO WITH THE TIME THAT IS
GIVEN US.

— J.R.R. Tolkien

SOUVENIR CLUTCH

HISTORICAL MARKER

We took our first big family road trip from Texas up to Washington, D.C. and back again during the summer of 2018. Our daughters were excited about packing their bags, staying in hotels, and seeing the sights, but mostly they were all about the souvenirs. Whether you find them on a trip abroad or a walk through your own hometown, this little clutch makes a great spot to stash your favorite mementos.

SCENIC ROUTE

A rainbow doesn't always have to take the ROYGBIV route. Sometimes leaving out a color or two from the traditional spectrum works better. Use your favorite fussy cuts for the feature squares and pair them with lighter half-square triangles against a low volume background for a clutch that's equal parts sweet and sassy.

FINISHED SIZE: 6˝ x 9˝

1 Use the B and D squares to make 12 HSTs according to the directions on page 28. Trim to 2" square, if necessary.

2 Referencing the Assembly Diagram, arrange the assembled HSTs from Step 1 along with the A and C squares into a 4 × 6 grid.

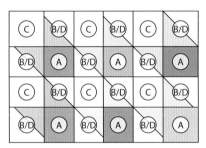

Assembly Diagram

3 Sew the squares into four rows. Press the seams in each row to opposites sides. Nest the seams (see page 27) for each row. Sew the rows together to form a Patchwork panel that measures 6½" × 9½".

4 Following the manufacturer's instructions, apply basting spray to the wrong side of the Patchwork panel and layer the Batting on top. Quilt as desired.

5 Repeat Step 4 with the remaining Batting and the Exterior Back rectangle.

6 Finish the pouch by following the assembly instructions on page 31 using the Exterior and Lining rectangles.

7 Thread the leather lacing through the zipper. Knot. Trim the ends at matching angles.

ROTARY CLUB

From the Focus Fabrics, cut:

(1) 2" square from each print (A)

From 6 Lighter Prints that coordinate with the A prints, cut:

(1) 2½" square from each print (B)

From the Exterior Back Fabric, cut:

(1) 6½" × 9½" rectangle

From a fat quarter of Batting and Lining Fabric, cut:

(2) 6½" × 9½" rectangles

From a fat quarter of the Background Fabric, cut:

(6) 2" squares (C)
(6) 2½" squares (D)

ADDITIONAL SUPPLIES

- Adhesive basting spray
- Turning tool
- Binding clips
- (1) 10" zipper
- (1) 7" length of leather lacing

Bookmobile Sleeve

HISTORICAL MARKER

We're all big readers in my family. I probably spent half my childhood in the town library just a few blocks from my house, checking out books at least once a week and reading them voraciously. Mysteries were my favorite — I couldn't get enough of Nancy Drew and the Boxcar Children. To this day, I love nothing more than to escape into a new book, which just goes to show that the best vacation might actually be a great story. With this case for your favorite electronic reading device, you'll always have a good read close by when you need it.

SCENIC ROUTE

Making fussy cut half-square triangles this small that stand on point can be tricky. So be sure to carefully check your pieces as you cut them out and sew them together. Using dark and light color pairs for the half-square triangles adds a nice contrast to the patchwork on this piece.

FINISHED SIZE: 5½" x 7½" closed

1 Referencing Figure 1 for color placement, use the A squares to make 8 HSTs following the directions on page 28. Trim HSTs to 1¾˝ square and arrange as shown.

2 Sew the pieces together into four rows, pressing the seams of each row in alternate directions. Then sew the rows together. Nest the seams (see page 27) of the HSTs to ensure that the final patchwork piece is centered correctly.

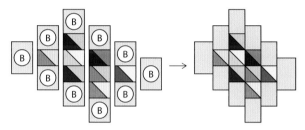

Figure 1

3 Trim the assembled unit from Step 2 to 4¼˝ × 6˝, centering the HSTs with about a ⅜˝ border around the outside. Sew C strips to the long sides of the front panel and press. Sew D strips to the top and bottom edges of the front panel and press.

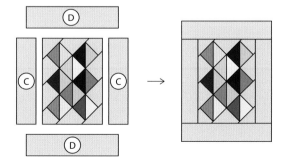

Figure 2

ROTARY CLUB

HALF-SQUARE TRIANGLES (HSTs)

From 16 scraps of various Feature Prints, at least 2˝ square, in 8 dark/light color pairs, cut:

  (1) 2˝ square from each print, being sure to cut on point if the print is a directional fabric (A)

From a fat quarter of Beige Denim, cut:

  (10) 1¾˝ × 2½˝ rectangles (B)

  (2) 1⅜˝ × 6˝ rectangles (C)

  (2) 1½˝ × 6˝ rectangles (D)

  (1) 6˝ × 8˝ rectangle (E)

From a fat quarter of Batting and Lining Fabric, cut:

  (2) 6˝ × 8˝ rectangles

ADDITIONAL SUPPLIES

- Adhesive basting spray
- Turning tool
- Binding clips
- Hair elastic
- (1) 1˝ button
- Hand sewing kit (see page 29)

④ Following the manufacturer's instructions, apply basting spray to the wrong side of the Front panel. Layer a Batting rectangle on top. Quilt as desired. Repeat with the Backing rectangle and the remaining Batting rectangle, but leave this unit unquilted.

⑤ Cut the hair elastic, being sure to remove any metal hardware if present and fold in half with the cut ends pinched together. Referencing Figure 3, center the cut ends along a short edge of the Backing rectangle, aligning the raw edges. Baste in place using a ⅛″ seam allowance.

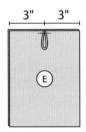

3"   3"

Figure 3

⑥ With the Front and Backing RST, use the binding clips to hold all of the layers together. Sew along the sides and the bottom edge, leaving the top edge with the elastic open. Clip the two bottom corners to reduce the bulk.

⑦ Repeat Step 6 with the Lining rectangles, but leave a 3″ gap in the lower short edge for turning.

⑧ Turn the Assembled Exterior from Step 6 right side out. Slip the Exterior inside the assembled Lining from Step 7. The right sides should be facing. Align the side seams and top raw edges of all of the layers and sew all around the circumference of the top opening. Ensure that the elastic is tucked down between the layers.

⑨ Reach in through the gap in the Lining to pull out the Exterior. Use a turning tool to gently push out the corners. Tuck the raw edges of the opening inside the gap and stitch about ⅛″ from the fold along the short edge, closing the gap in the process.

⑩ Push the Lining inside the Exterior and press well. Edgestitch around the opening of the sleeve. Fold over the elastic and make a mark in the middle of where the loop forms. Center the button on the mark on the Exterior Front and sew in place by hand being sure not to stitch through to the Lining.

DETOUR

This project can be easily sized up or down for any electronic device you want to protect: cell phones, tablets, laptops, or even handheld games. Just measure your device and adjust the cut measurements as needed, taking seam allowances and batting thickness into consideration.

Curio Pocket

HISTORICAL MARKER

My grandmother was the queen of collectors. She loved taking my sister and me to her favorite antique shops, always slipping us each a $5 bill so that we could find a "treasure" to bring home. Now my girls are following in her footsteps, collecting everything from buttons to rocks to postcards. I, of course, collect sewing notions, and this pocket is the perfect spot in which to keep my favorite things.

SCENIC ROUTE

Tiny fussy cuts make for sweet banners on each of these pockets. I adore this moody shade of blue for the pocket, which looks perfectly retro against a vintage newspaper background.

FINISHED SIZE: 5½" × 7"

FABRIC	FOR	CUTTING
5˝ square of 4 different Focal Prints	BANNERS	(1) 1½˝ × 2˝ rectangle from each print (A) (2) 1˝ squares from each print (B)
Newspaper Print	MAIN PANEL	(1) 6˝ × 8½˝ rectangle (C)
10˝ square of Blue Dot Print	POCKET BACKGROUND	(4) 1˝ × 1½˝ rectangles (D) (2) 1˝ × 2½˝ rectangles (E) (3) 1½˝ × 2½˝ rectangles (F) (2) 1˝ × 8½˝ rectangles (G) (1) 3½˝ × 8½˝ rectangle (H)
10˝ square of Peach Floral Print	POCKET BINDING	(1) 2˝ × 8½˝ rectangle (I)
	MAIN PANEL BACKING	(1) 6˝ × 8½˝ rectangle (J)
10˝ square of Batting	MAIN PANEL INTERFACING	(1) 6˝ × 8½˝ rectangle (K)
	POCKET INTERFACING	(1) 3½˝ × 8½˝ rectangle (L)

ADDITIONAL SUPPLIES

- (1) 2˝ length of ⅝˝ wide twill tape • Adhesive basting spray • Turning tool • Binding clips
- Hand sewing kit (see page 29)

❶ Make four flying geese units using the B and D pieces. Line up a B square on the right side of a D rectangle with the RST and sew on the diagonal line from the top inside corner to the lower outside corner. Trim the seam to ¼˝ away from the sewn line and press the square open. Repeat on the other side of the rectangle with a second B square (Fig. 1). Repeat for all four rectangles and pairs of squares.

❷ Sew an A rectangle to the upper edge of each coordinating flying geese unit from Step 1.

❸ Referencing Figure 2, arrange an E rectangle, then three alternating Banner/F rectangle pairs and finish with another E rectangle. Sew together all of the pieces into a 2½˝ × 8½˝ rectangle and press well.

Figure 1

4 Sew a G strip to both long edges of the assembled unit from Step 3 (Fig. 2). Following the manufacturer's instructions, apply basting spray to the wrong side of the Exterior Pocket panel and to the wrong side of the H Background rectangle. Sandwich the L batting rectangle between the two sides of the Assembled Pocket. Quilt as desired.

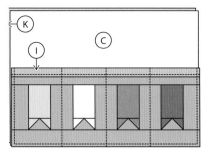

Figure 3

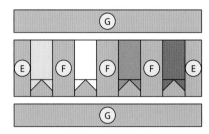

Figure 2

5 Use the I strip to bind the upper edge of the Pocket in the same manner as you would bind a quilt.

6 Apply basting spray to the wrong side of the C rectangle and layer the K Batting on top. Turn over so that piece C is right side up. Place the Pocket from Step 5 on top, aligning the raw edges on the bottom long edge of the C rectangle. Baste in place along the three sides using a ⅛″ seam allowance.

7 Referencing Figure 3, divide the Pocket into four slots by stitching three lines where indicated. Be sure to stop stitching and backstitch at the top of the Pocket binding.

8 Fold the twill tape in half with the WST so the short ends meet. Position the tab just above the top edge of one side of the Pocket on the right side of the Main Exterior, aligning the raw edges. Baste in place using a ⅛″ seam allowance.

9 Layer the J Backing rectangle on top of the assembled unit from Step 7, RST. Make sure the tab is nested inside the layers and attach binding clips around the perimeter to prevent the layers from shifting. Stitch around the rectangle. Leave a 3″-4″ gap in the top edge for turning and backstitch at the start and finish of the stitching line. Clip the corners to reduce the bulk.

10 Turn the piece right side out, gently pushing out the corners with a turning tool. Tuck the raw edges around the opening into the gap from Step 8, press and edgestitch around three sides of the exposed Main Exterior (not on the Pocket) to finish.

DETOUR

Add a loop at the top for instant hanging storage or sew an elastic/button closure on the sides so that you can roll up your pocket and take it with you when you are on-the-go.

Beachcomber Drawstring Bag

HISTORICAL MARKER

I've spent countless hours walking by the ocean over the years. Shells, pebbles, bits of driftwood—there's always something pretty lying in the sand. This project makes a lovely reusable gift wrapping for small presents, but it's also a fun bag for little ones who can easily work the opening to keep their treasures inside.

SCENIC ROUTE

I couldn't resist playing along with the name for this one, pulling prints in shades of the ocean for all my fussy cut rectangles. Mimic the sea again by arranging your colors so that they intensify from top to bottom. Low volume prints colored in orange and gold are a nice contrast, as is a narrow striped denim for the accents.

FINISHED SIZE: 5˝ x 8˝ closed

1 Referencing Figure 1, arrange the 30 A rectangles into (2) 5 × 3 grids. Sew each into five rows and then sew the rows together, being sure to press the seams in opposite directions for each row.

2 Following the manufacturer's instructions, apply basting spray to the wrong side of an assembled Patchwork panel from Step 1. Center a Batting rectangle in the middle of the panel and align the side raw edges. There should be 2″ of Batting exposed above and below the Patchwork. Quilt as desired. Repeat with the other Patchwork panel and Batting rectangle.

3 With a B rectangle and an assembled unit from Step 2 RST, sew together along the bottom long edge. Fold the unsewn long edge of the B rectangle back onto the Batting, pressing and then applying another layer of basting spray. Topstitch ⅛″ above and below seam. Repeat with the other Patchwork panel and another B rectangle.

Figure 1

4 Hem the 4″ sides of a C rectangle by folding them in ¼″, WST. Topstitch ⅛″ from each fold. Fold in half lengthwise with the WST. Center the raw ends on the long edge of a remaining B rectangle and baste in place. Topstitch along the folded edge of the casing loop to secure it in place on the B rectangle, ⅛″ from fold. Repeat.

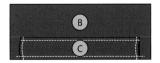

Figure 2

ROTARY CLUB

From 5″ square each of 15 different Prints in shades of blue and white, cut:
(2) 1½″ × 2½″ rectangles from each print (A)

From a fat quarter of Indigo Denim, cut:
(4) 2½″ × 6½″ rectangles (B)
(2) 4″ × 6″ rectangles (C)

From a fat quarter of Plaid Print, cut:
(2) 6½″ × 9½″ rectangles (E)

From the Batting, cut:
(2) 6½″ × 9½″ rectangles

ADDITIONAL SUPPLIES

- (2) 24″ lengths of ⅛″ wide cording
- Adhesive basting spray
- Binding clips
- Turning tool
- Marking tool
- Safety pin

⑤ Position the basted edge of the assembled unit from Step 4 along the long edge of the unsewn side of the Patchwork panel from Step 3, RST. Stitch together and then press the B/C piece back onto the Batting, pressing and then fusing with adhesive basting spray. Topstitch ⅛˝ below the seam on the Patchwork panel. Repeat with the remaining pieces. Trim both full assembled Exterior pieces to 6½˝ x 9½˝, if needed. (Fig. 3)

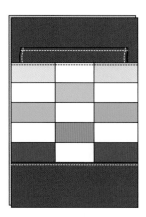

Figure 3

⑥ Place the Exterior pieces RST and sew along the sides and lower edge, backstitching at the start and finish and leaving the top open. Carefully cut a 1½˝ square out of both lower corners of the B rectangle without the casing.

⑦ To box the corners (see the diagram for the Boardwalk Mini Tote on page 52), pinch and nest together the side and lower seams where the square

in Step 6 was cut out. Stitch across the raw edges at least twice for extra strength. Repeat with the other corner and then turn the Exterior right side out.

⑧ Repeat Steps 6-7 with the Lining rectangles (E), leaving a 2˝ gap in the lower edge of the Lining for turning later. Leave the Lining inside out.

⑨ Slip the Exterior inside the Lining with the RST, checking that the side seams align. Use binding clips to hold both units together, then stitch around the circumference of the opening.

⑩ Pull the Exterior out through gap in the Lining, pushing out the corners of bag with a turning tool and pressing carefully. Tuck the seam allowances of the opening inside the gap in the Lining. Press, and stitch closed about ⅛˝ - ¹⁄₁₆˝ from edge. Push the Lining down into the Exterior.

⑪ Edgestitch around the top of the bag opening to finish. Tie one end of the cording to a closed safety pin and use it to thread through one casing loop, around the side, and through the remaining loop. Knot the ends together. Repeat with the other length of cording, starting from the other side of the bag (Fig. 4). Trim the cording ends as needed.

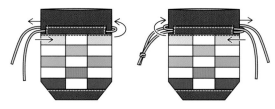

Figure 4

HOBBY KIT

HISTORICAL MARKER

I'm absolutely crazy about little sewing kits. They're small, handy and completely adorable. I not only take them with me on the go, but I also keep one in our bedroom, where I've spent many an evening hand stitching a project while James and I enjoy an old movie together after we've put the girls to bed.

SCENIC ROUTE

Try using solid colors for the flowers on the cover of this kit to help the diagonal line of fussy cut squares stand out. Linen has enough structure for the main body and is a nice backdrop for the other prints. Feel free to embellish this kit with extra buttons and trims if you like.

⚙ ROTARY CLUB

FABRIC	FOR	CUTTING
5″ square of Sunshine Print		Fussy cut (see page 27) into (3) 1½″ squares (A)
5″ square of Solid Pink Print		(4) 1½″ squares (B)
Dark Pink Print		(1) 1½″ square (C)
5″ square of Yellow Print		(4) 1½″ squares (D)
Gold Solid	FLAP	(1) 1½″ square (E)
10″ square of Cream Dot Print		(2) 1½″ squares (F) (2) 1½″ × 2½″ rectangles (G) (2) 1½″ × 3½″ rectangles (H) (1) 1½″ × 5½″ rectangle (I)
Music Print	FLAP LINING	(1) 5½″ × 6½″ rectangle (J)
Fat quarter of Brown Denim	MAIN BODY	(2) 7″ × 15″ rectangles (K)
Cream Floral Print	LARGE INNER POCKET	(1) 10″ × 15″ rectangle (L)
Pink Geometric Print	NEEDLE LANDING SPOT	(1) 2½″ × 4¼″ rectangle (M)

ADDITIONAL CUTTING AND SUPPLIES

FABRIC	CUTTING	SUPPLIES
Batting	(1) 7″ × 9″ rectangle (1) 7″ × 15″ rectangle	• (1) 7″ length of ½″ wide ruler twill tape • (1) 2″ length of ¾″ wide berry basket twill tape
Pink Floral Fabric and the Muslin	(1) 2 × 16″ rectangle of each for the strap	• Adhesive basting spray • Turning tool • Binding clips
Double-Sided Fusible Interfacing	(1) 2½″ × 4¼″ rectangle	• (1) ¾″ button • Hair elastic
Scrap of Cream Felt	(1) 2″ × 3¾″ rectangle of each for the strap	• Hand sewing kit (see page 29) *Optional: Scallop pinking shears

ASSEMBLING THE FLAP

① Referencing Figure 1, arrange the A-I units as shown. Sew the center squares together into a 9-Patch, first pressing the seams in opposite directions in each row prior to assembly. Next sew the two pieces for the right and left edges together and sew them to the 9-Patch. Assemble the units in Rows 2 and 4 and press. Finally, sew Rows 1 and 2 together and attach to the central panel and Row 4 to the bottom of the assembled unit. Press the Flap panel well.

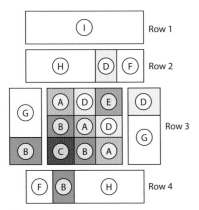

Figure 1

② Following the manufacturer's instructions, apply basting spray to the wrong side of the assembled Flap from Step 1 and layer the smaller Batting rectangle on top. Quilt as desired. Trim the panel to 5½″ × 6½″.

③ With the assembled unit from Step 2 and the J rectangle RST, clip together with binding clips to secure the layers. Stitch around three sides leaving the long edge of the I rectangle unsewn. Trim the corners to reduce the bulk, turn right side out, push out the corners with a turning tool and press. Edgestitch around three sides, still leaving the top unsewn. Set aside.

ASSEMBLING THE POCKET

① Fold and press the L rectangle in half lengthwise with the WST and edgestitch along the fold. Position the pocket on the long edge of a K rectangle. Baste in place along the sides and lower long edge. Referencing Figure 2, stitch two vertical lines on the pocket panel 4½″ from each short edge. Be sure not to go beyond the pocket fold and backstitch at the start and finish of the line of stitching. Set aside until Step 7 on the facing page.

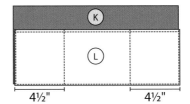

Figure 2

② Referencing Figure 3 on the facing page, position the 7″ length of twill tape 2″ away from the left short edge of the second K rectangle. Baste in place along the short ends of the tape using a ⅛″ seam allowance. Stitch horizontal lines across the twill tape every ⅞″ to create slots for binding clips, mini pencils or tools. Be sure to backstitch at the start and finish of each line of stitching and ensure that you are sewing through both of the layers.

③ Following the manufacturer's instructions, fuse the rectangle of Interfacing to the wrong side of the M rectangle. If desired, trim the edges with scallop pinking shears (otherwise the edges will fray nicely if that is preferred). Referencing Figure 3, center the M rectangle, 1″ away from the right short edge and fuse to the K rectangle. Center the Felt rectangle on top of the M rectangle and pin in place. Edgestitch around the perimeter of the Felt through all of the layers to secure them in place.

④ Fold the short length of twill tape in half with the WST and position the tape in the middle of the right short edge of the K rectangle. Align the raw edges and baste in place using a ⅛″ seam allowance.

⑤ Cut the hair elastic, being sure to remove any metal hardware if necessary, and fold in half. Center on the bottom edge of the K rectangle and align the raw edges. Baste in place using a ⅛″ seam allowance.

⑥ Referencing Figure 3, position a pin 4½″ away from each short side on the top edge of the K rectangle.

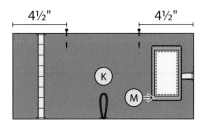

Figure 3

⑦ With the two assembled K rectangles RST, use binding clips to keep the layers together. Ensure that the elastic and short twill tape tab are sandwiched between the layers. Sew around the perimeter of the rectangles through all of the layers and leave a gap between the pins from Step 6.

⑧ Trim the corners to reduce the bulk, and turn the assembled unit right side out through the gap from Step 7. Push out the corners using a chopstick or similar blunt object. Press well.

ASSEMBLING AND ATTACHING THE STRAP TO THE FLAP

① Following the manufacturer's instructions, apply basting spray to the wrong side of the Muslin and position the Strap rectangle WST. Follow the directions on page 32 to make a strap.

② Fold the assembled Strap from Step 1 in half so the short raw ends meet. Baste the two ends of the Strap together using a ⅛″ seam allowance.

③ Position the Strap along the patchwork Flap ⅛″ away from the left side and aligning the raw edges of the Strap with upper raw edge of the assembled Flap. The length of the Strap should be laying on the front of the Flap and extending past the opposite finished short edge. Baste the Strap in place using a ⅛″ seam allowance being sure to stitch through all of the layers.

FINISHING

1 Carefully tuck the raw edges of the assembled Pocket panel inside the opening between the pins of the K rectangle. Press well to tuck in the raw edges of the seam allowance WST.

2 Referencing Figure 4 and with the Pockets and Flap lining both facing up, slip the assembled Strap/Flap unit inside the opening in the Pocket panel by about ½". Pin in place to prevent shift and edgestitch around the perimeter of the Pocket panel, closing the gap and securing the Flap and Strap in place in the process.

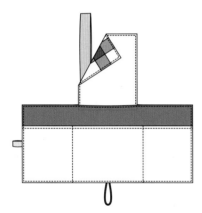

Figure 4

3 Press the entire unit. Fold in each side of the Pocket Panel to form a trifold, then fold the Flap over the trifold. Bring up the elastic loop and mark the center. Hand stitch the button on the front of the Flap over the mark and fill up your case with sewing goodies before you head out the door.

SCOUT'S HONOR PENCIL CASE

HISTORICAL MARKER

My family went camping only twice when I was growing up, and both trips were plagued with bad weather and countless mishaps. After that my dad liked to joke that our family did all our camping in hotels. Still, I've always been fascinated by vintage scouting and camping paraphernalia. The fussy cut "badges" on this pencil case are a fun way to get a taste of the scouting scene . . . no bug spray required.

SCENIC ROUTE

Honestly, the best part is making up stories about the "badges" based on the fabrics you pick, so choose your prints accordingly. Yarn dyed linen for the exterior and plaid lining are a perfect fit for the theme.

FINISHED BLOCK SIZE: 2″ square
FINISHED SIZE: 3½″ × 9″

ROTARY CLUB

FABRIC	FOR	CUTTING
Scraps of 3 Novelty Prints	BADGE CENTERS	Fussy cut (see page 27) (1) 2″ square from each print (A)
10″ square of 3 Coordinating Solid Fabrics	BADGE BORDERS	(2) ¾″ × 2″ rectangles from each solid (B) (2) ¾″ × 2½″ rectangles from each solid (C) (1) 1½″ square from each solid (D)
Fat quarter of Gray Linen	BACKGROUND FRONT PANEL	(12) 1″ squares (E) (4) 1¼″ × 2½″ rectangles (F) (2) 9½″ × 1¼″ rectangles (G)
	BACK PANEL	(1) 9½″ × 4″ rectangle (H)
10″ square of Plaid Print	LINING	(2) 9½″ × 4″ rectangles (I)

ADDITIONAL SUPPLIES

- (2) 9½″ × 4″ rectangles of batting • (1) 2½″ length of ⅝″ twill tape • (1) 9″ zipper
- (1) 5″ length of leather lacing (optional) • Adhesive basting spray • Turning tool • Binding clips

❶ Sort the A–E fabric cuts into 3 groups, 1 set for each badge.

❷ Sew a B strip to the right and left edges of the A square, press, then sew a C strip to the upper and lower edges of the unit and press again. Use the instructions on page 32 and the D and E squares and press. (Fig. 1)

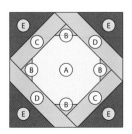

Figure 1

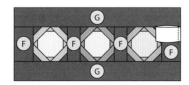

Figure 2

❸ Referencing Figure 2, alternate F rectangles and completed Badge blocks. Sew the units together in a row and press.

❹ Sew the G rectangles to the two long edges of the assembled unit from Step 3. Following the manufacturer's instructions, apply basting spray to the wrong side of the Front panel and layer the Batting rectangle on top. Quilt as desired.

❺ Fold the twill tape in half with the WST and place on the right side of the Front panel about 1″ away from the top right corner. Align the raw edges and baste through all of the layers using a ⅛″ seam allowance. (Fig. 2)

❻ Use the remaining fabrics to finish the zipper pouch by following the assembly directions on page 31.

COLOR BOOK

HISTORICAL MARKER

My oldest daughter's first book was a small cloth volume about the Christmas story, and we read it a zillion times. I loved that I never had to worry about it getting damaged or having her dissolve any paper in her mouth. If you're looking for an original baby shower gift or birthday present for a young child, this is it.

SCENIC ROUTE

Projects for young children are the best places to use your novelty prints. It's up to you how you want to organize your book. You can assign a different color or theme to each page or be completely random in your choices. Try using fabrics from a single designer for all your feature prints so that your book really looks as if it had a single illustrator.

FINISHED SIZE: 4½″ square, closed

ROTARY CLUB

FABRIC	FOR	CUTTING
5˝ square Alphabet Print		(1) 2˝ square (A)
5˝ square Orange Gingham Print		(4) 1˝ × 2˝ rectangles (B)
10˝ square White Solid		(4) 1˝ × 2˝ rectangles (C) (8) 1˝ squares (D)
5˝ square Yellow Floral Print	COVER	(4) 1½˝ squares (E)
5˝ square Green Star Print		(2) 1˝ × 4˝ rectangles (F) (2) 5˝ × 1˝ rectangles (G)
10˝ square Pink Grid Print		(1) 5˝ × 5½˝ rectangle (H)
24 scraps, of Colorful Prints (I used 4 each in pink, orange, yellow, green, blue, and purple)	PAGES	(1) 2½˝ square from each print (I)
10˝ square of Text Print	BOOK LINING	(2) 5˝ × 5¼˝ rectangles (J)

ADDITIONAL SUPPLIES

- (1) 5½˝ × 10½˝ rectangle of batting • (3) 3½˝ squares of lightweight woven interfacing or muslin
- Adhesive basting spray • Turning tool • Binding clips

ASSEMBLING THE EXTERIOR

1 With the WST, sew together a B and C rectangle along one long side. Press open. Repeat to create a total of four units.

2 Following the instructions on page 32, use two D squares to snowball opposite corners of each E square. Press open.

3 Referencing Figure 1, arrange the A square as well as the assembled units from Steps 1 and 2 into a 3 × 3, sew together and press. Attach an F rectangle to the two sides and press. Finally, attach the remaining longer G rectangles to the upper and lower edges and press again.

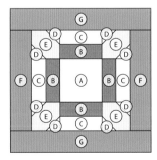

Figure 1

4 Sew the short edge of the H rectangle to the left edge of the assembled unit from Step 3 and press. Apply basting spray to the wrong side of the Exterior panel and center the batting rectangle on top. Quilt as desired. Trim down to 5˝ × 10˝.

ASSEMBLING THE INTERIOR PAGES

1 Divide the I squares into six color groups of four each. Sew each block together into a 4-Patch. Press.

DETOUR

If you are using a series of single 4½″ square images, skip Step 1 and go straight to Step 2.

2 Separate the 4-Patch blocks or 4″ squares into three pairs. Place one pair RST and sew along three edges, leaving open the side that will be inserted into the book spine. Backstitch at the start and finish. Trim the corners. Turn the page right side out, gently pushing out the corners with a turning tool. Press. Slip a Muslin or Interfacing square inside the page and edgestitch around the perimeter. (Fig. 2)

Figure 2

3 Repeat Step 2 with the remaining two pair of pages.

4 Stack the assembled 4-Patch square pages in the desired order from top to bottom and baste together along the open raw edges using a ⅛″ seam allowance. I recommend starting at the middle and sewing to each corner so that the pages stay in place.

5 Stack the inside of the book together by positioning one J Lining rectangle right side up. Layer the assembled stack from Step 4 with the last page facing down. Finally, layer the second J Lining rectangle wrong side up. Be sure that the raw edges of the stack align with the short edge of the Linings before stitching together. Use binding clips to prevent the layers from shifting. Beginning in the middle of the right short raw edge, sew the layers together towards one long edge, then repeat.

6 Open the assembled Lining panel from Step 4 so that it lies flat with all of the 4-Patch pages to one side. Place the Exterior panel on top of the Lining, RST and clip or pin them together.

7 Sew around the perimeter, leaving a 3″ gap along one side for turning and backstitching at the start and finish of the line of stitching. Trim the corners to reduce the bulk and turn the book right side out through the gap.

8 Using a turning tool, gently push out the corners. Tuck the raw edges inside the gap and press. Edgestitch around the perimeter, closing the gap in the process. Close the book and press.

 TOUR GUIDE

Both times you approach the book's "spine" (halfway along the long side of the book) when edgestitching in Step 7, keep the needle down in the fabric, lift up the presser foot, and carefully flip the pages under the book so that the raw edges are facing away from you and behind the needle before you continue stitching. This will make it easier to get a neat line of stitching around the entire book.

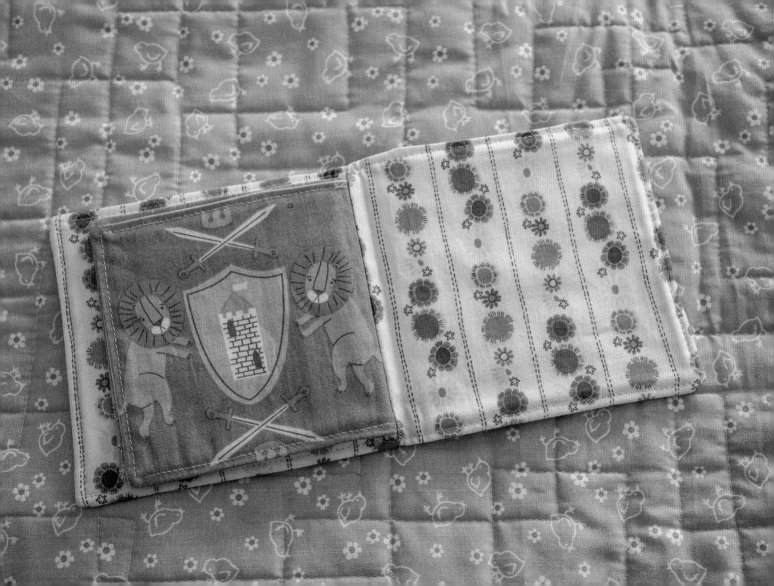

HISTORICAL MARKER

Back when my husband and I were newlyweds, we spent every Saturday morning at the laundromat up the street. James bought a brown vinyl coin pouch to keep in his glove box, and we were constantly on the lookout for quarters to stash inside it so we could keep those machines running. I like to think that I wouldn't have loathed doing laundry quite so much if I'd had a coin pouch as cute as this one.

SCENIC ROUTE

If you've never attempted hexagons before, this project is a great way to start. I chose 3 eye-catching prints that I wanted to feature in the center and surrounded them with coordinating blenders. Pay careful attention to what will be trimmed away as you arrange your hexagons so that your favorite details make it onto the pouch.

FINISHED SIZE: 3¾˝ × 5˝

1. Referencing Making Hexagons (see page 30), baste all of the A squares using the 1˝ hexagon paper templates. Create a total of 12 basted hexagons.

2. Referencing Figure 1, arrange the hexagons as shown. Sew the hexagons together in four vertical columns of three hexagons each and then hand sew the columns together.

Figure 1

3. Remove the basting threads and paper pieces, and press the assembled Exterior well. Following the manufacturer's instructions, apply basting spray to the wrong side of the assembled Exterior and center the Batting on top. Quilt as desired. Trim to 4¼˝ × 5½˝.

4. Fold the twill tape in half with the WST. Position the tape ¾˝ below the upper left edge of the Exterior, aligning the raw edges. Baste in place using a ⅛˝ seam allowance.

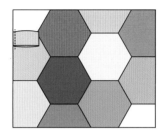

Figure 2

5. Apply basting spray to the wrong side of the Backing rectangle and center the Batting on top. Quilt as desired. Trim to 4¼˝ × 5½˝.

6. Finish the zipper pouch following instructions on page 31.

 TOUR GUIDE

Keep a basket filled with hexagon paper pieces, the supplies in the hand sewing kit from page 29 and pretty scraps of fabric. Whenever you're in the mood to do projects like this one, all you need to do is grab the basket and go!

 **ROTARY CLUB**

HEXAGONS

Scraps of 12 various prints, cut:

(1) 3˝ square from each print (A)

ADDITIONAL SUPPLIES

- (2) 4¾˝ × 6˝ rectangles of Batting
- (1) 4¼˝ × 5½˝ rectangle of Backing fabric
- (2) 4¼˝ × 5½˝ rectangles of Lining fabric
- (1) 2˝ length of ⅝˝ wide twill tape
- Adhesive basting spray
- Binding clips
- Turning tool
- (1) 7˝ zipper
- 12 copies of the 1˝ hexagon template (see page 30)
- Hand sewing kit (see page 29)

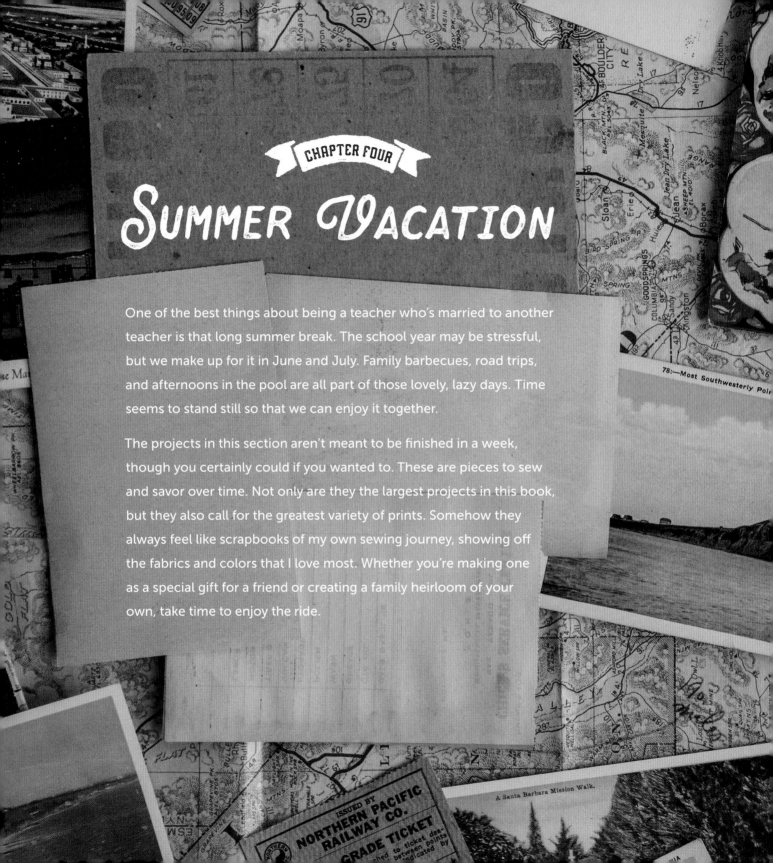

CHAPTER FOUR

SUMMER VACATION

One of the best things about being a teacher who's married to another teacher is that long summer break. The school year may be stressful, but we make up for it in June and July. Family barbecues, road trips, and afternoons in the pool are all part of those lovely, lazy days. Time seems to stand still so that we can enjoy it together.

The projects in this section aren't meant to be finished in a week, though you certainly could if you wanted to. These are pieces to sew and savor over time. Not only are they the largest projects in this book, but they also call for the greatest variety of prints. Somehow they always feel like scrapbooks of my own sewing journey, showing off the fabrics and colors that I love most. Whether you're making one as a special gift for a friend or creating a family heirloom of your own, take time to enjoy the ride.

WHAT YOU DO MAKES A DIFFERENCE AND YOU HAVE TO DECIDE WHAT KIND OF DIFFERENCE YOU WANT TO MAKE.

— JANE GOODALL

FIREWORKS PILLOW

HISTORICAL MARKER

Nothing says summer like an old-fashioned fireworks display. Two weeks after we moved to Texas, we took our daughters to a nearby Fourth of July event, settling down on the grass in front of the local high school with all the other families from town. Watching their faces light up in awe as the show started is something I'll never forget. These blocks remind me so much of those colorful explosions in the sky.

TOUR GUIDE

Using three fabrics in varying degrees of the same color gives depth to the block and turns a spotlight on the center print. Highlight the center even more by using solids for the outer fabrics.

FINISHED BLOCK SIZE: 5″ square

FINISHED PILLOW SIZE: 16″ square

ROTARY CLUB

FABRIC	FOR	CUTTING
5″ square each of 9 Feature Prints in Light Raspberry, Pink, Light Red, Peach, Pale Yellow, Light Green, Light Blue, Light Aqua and Lavender	CENTER CROSS	(1) 3½″ × 1½″ rectangle from each print (A) (2) 1½″ squares from each print (B)
10″ square each of 9 Solid Fabrics, a shade darker than each color listed above	DIAGONAL LINES FOR CORNERS	(4) 2½″ squares from each (C)
5″ square each of 9 Solid Fabrics, the darkest shade of each color listed above	SQUARES AT THE ENDS OF THE CROSS	(4) 1½″ squares from each (D)
½ yard of White Solid	SNOWBALL SQUARES	(72) 1½″ squares (E)
	SASHING STRIPS	(6) 1″ × 5½″ rectangles (F) (2) 16½″ × 1″ rectangles (G)
½ yard of White Silverware Print	PILLOW ENVELOPE CLOSURE	(2) 12½″ × 16½″ rectangles (H)

ADDITIONAL SUPPLIES

- (1) 20″ square of batting and lining fabric
- (1) 16″ square pillow form
- Adhesive basting spray
- Turning tool

ASSEMBLING THE BLOCKS

1 Separate the A-D fabric cuts by block, so that the correct colors are together for a total of nine blocks. Referencing the instructions on page 32, use the E squares to snowball opposite corners of the four C squares for each block and press.

2 With the RST, sew together the A rectangle and two D squares for each block along their short edges and press. With the RST, sew the B and remaining D squares together. Keep directionality in mind. Referencing Figure 1, arrange into three rows. With the RST, sew the units together and then sew rows together pressing the seams for each row in opposite directions.

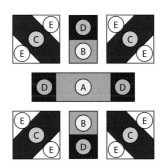

Figure 1

3 Repeat Steps 1-2 for all 9 of the blocks.

ASSEMBLING THE PILLOW TOP

1 Arrange the assembled blocks into a 3 × 3 grid. Sew F rectangles on either side of the center block of each row, then sew the side blocks to 3 horizontal rows. Press the seams open and Sew G strips between the rows. Sew the three assembled rows together to finish the pillow top. Press. (Fig. 2)

Figure 2

2 Following the manufacturer's instructions, apply basting spray to the wrong side of the assembled pillow top from Step 1. Layer the Batting square and apply another layer of basting spray. Layer the Lining square right side up and quilt as desired. Trim to 16½″ square.

3 With the WST, fold a short end of an H rectangle by ⅜″ and press. Fold over ⅜″ again and press. Topstitch ¼″ away from the fold. Repeat for the second Backing rectangle.

4 With the assembled pillow top right side up, layer an assembled H rectangle from Step 3 wrong side facing up and aligning the raw edges. Repeat with the second H rectangle aligning the raw edges with the opposite side of the pillow top. The Backing rectangles will overlap. Sew around the perimeter.

5 Trim the corners to reduce the bulk, turn right side out and gently push out the corners with a chopstick or similar blunt object. Press well and insert the pillow form.

Floss Mini Quilt

HISTORICAL MARKER

When Aurifil Thread debuted their floss several years back, I was so taken with those wooden spools of color that I immediately sat down and designed this quilt. You'll notice that all the spool colors are added into the binding on the left edge of the quilt except for the empty one which is represented by the scrap on the lower right. And yes, I had to quilt this project by hand—in Aurifloss, of course.

TOUR GUIDE

When choosing fabrics for the spools, I love mixing in some special fussy cut prints along with the blenders. Graph paper inspired fabric adds a nice texture to the background.

FINISHED BLOCK SIZE: 1½" x 4½"

FINISHED QUILT SIZE: 16¾" x 26"

 **ROTARY CLUB**

FABRIC	FOR	CUTTING
Fat quarter of Brown Stitch Print	SPOOL ENDS	(40) 1″ × 2″ rectangles (A)
	EMPTY SPOOL	(1) 1″ × 4″ rectangle (B)
Scraps of 19 Prints in various colors	THREAD PORTION OF SPOOLS	(1) 2″ × 4″ rectangle from each print (C)
	COLORED PORTION OF BINDING	(1) 1″ × 2″ rectangle from each print (D)
2½″ square of Orange Floral Print	COLORED PORTION OF BINDING	(1) 1″ × 2″ rectangle (E)
½ yard of Off-White Grid Print	EMPTY SPOOL	(2) 1″ × 4″ rectangles (F)
	BACKGROUND	(16) 1½″ × 5″ rectangles (G) (3) 12″ × 1½″ rectangles (H) (1) 2″ × 21½″ rectangle (I) (1) 13½″ × 2″ rectangle (J) (1) 3½″ × 23″ rectangle (K) (1) 16½″ × 3½″ rectangle (L)
⅓ yard of White Solid	BINDING	(1) 1″ × 2″ rectangle (M) (2) 2″ × 35″ rectangles (N) (1) 2″ × 8″ rectangle (O)

ADDITIONAL CUTTING AND SUPPLIES

FABRIC	CUTTING
Batting and Backing Fabric	(1) 21″ × 30″ rectangle of each

ASSEMBLING THE SPOOLS

1 With the RST, sew an A rectangle to both short ends of a C rectangle and press. Repeat for all 19 spools

2 With the RST, sew F rectangles to the long sides of the B rectangle and press. Sew the remaining two A rectangles to the short ends to complete the empty spool block and press.

ASSEMBLING THE QUILT TOP

1 Referencing the Quilt Top Assembly Diagram, arrange the assembled 20 spool blocks into a 5 x 4 grid as shown.

2 Place G rectangles between the blocks and stitch the blocks and rectangles together to form four rows of five spools each. Press the seams open.

3 Place an H rectangle between each of the rows. Sew the rows together and press.

4 Sew the I rectangle to the right edge of the assembled unit from Step 3 and press. Attach the J, K and L rectangles in the same way.

5 Layer the Backing rectangle wrong side up, the Batting rectangle and the quilt top right side up. Smooth out the layers and baste or pin if desired to secure all of the layers. Quilt as desired. Trim to 16½˝ x 26˝.

CREATING THE BINDING STRIPS

1 Sew the D rectangles together along their 2˝ sides in the same color order as the spools in the quilt (left to right, top to bottom), inserting the M rectangle for the empty spool.

2 Sew the N rectangles above and below the stack from Step 1, adding the E rectangle below the lower N rectangle and the O rectangle below E. Use this assembled strip to bind and finish the quilt, positioning the strip so that the colored stack starts 2½˝ below the upper left corner on the left edge of quilt.

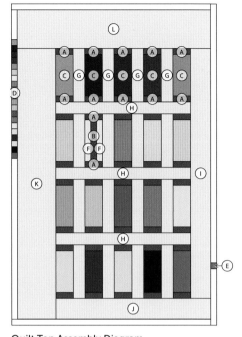

Quilt Top Assembly Diagram

DETOUR

This is a great project for the times when you want to show off a specific fabric collection, as I did in my prototype version of this quilt featuring Carkai by Carolyn Friedlander. Instead of using one fabric for the background, I tossed in some low volume prints from the collection along with solid white to make a scrappy backdrop with lots of texture.

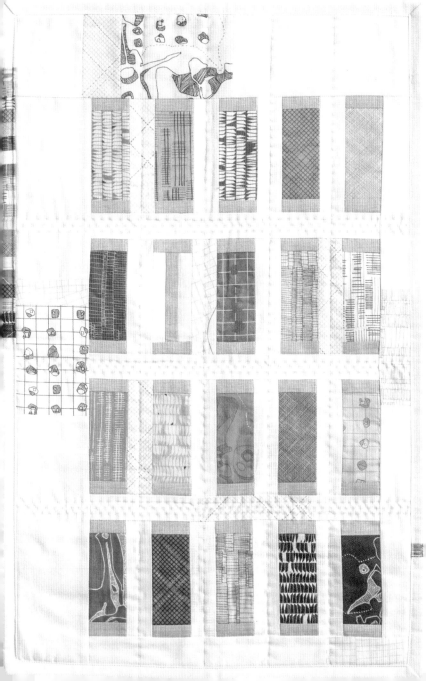

Palm Springs Bag

HISTORICAL MARKER

I've taken several vacations in Palm Springs with friends and family, and there's nothing like that famous desert resort to make you slow down and enjoy the sunshine . . . not too far from a swimming pool, of course. This bag is not just the perfect accessory for a weekend trip but also the perfect pastime. Hexagons are always my favorite sewing project to take along when I travel.

SCENIC ROUTE

Pastel prints are so cheerful in this hexagon panel, and I like to put a row of low volume prints down the middle to draw the eye there. The patchwork and starry lining contrast nicely with the soft gray denim. Boxy bags are my favorite, but they are definitely more challenging to make, so read through the directions carefully and take your time as you sew.

FINISHED SIZE: 5⅛″ × 7″ closed

FABRIC	FOR	CUTTING
Scraps from 17 Prints in pastel and low volume colors	HEXAGONS	(1) 3″ square from each print (A)
½ yard of Batting	FRONT POCKET	(1) 7¼″ × 11½″ rectangle (B) (1) 2″ × 9½″ rectangle (C)
	MAIN PANEL	(2) 7¼″ × 9½″ rectangles (D)
	ZIPPER PANEL	(2) 2″ × 13½″ rectangles (E)
	GUSSET EXTERIOR	(1) 3¾″ × 24½″ rectangle (F)
	INTERIOR POCKET	(1) 5¼″ × 9½″ rectangle (G)
½ yard of Gray Denim	FRONT POCKET	(2) 1½″ × 5¼″ rectangles (H) (1) 2″ × 9½″ rectangle (I)
	ZIPPER ENDS	(2) 1″ × 3″ rectangles (J)
	MAIN BACK PANEL EXTERIOR	(1) 7¼″ × 9½″ rectangle (K)
	ZIPPER PANEL EXTERIOR	(2) 2″ × 13½″ rectangles (L)
	GUSSET EXTERIOR	(1) 3¾″ × 24½″ strip (M)
	HANDLES	(2) 4″ × 12½″ strips (N)
½ yard of Star Print	FRONT POCKET LINING	(1) 5¼″ × 9½″ rectangle (O) (1) 2″ x 9½″ rectangle (P)
	MAIN PANEL AND FRONT POCKET LINING	(3) 7¼″ x 9½″ rectangles (Q)
	ZIPPER PANEL LINING	(2) 2″ x 13½″ strips (R)
	INTERIOR POCKET	(1) 9½″ x 10½″ rectangle (S)
	GUSSET LINING	(1) 3¾″ x 24½″ rectangle (T)
5″ square of Text Print	ZIPPER TABS	(2) 2″ x 2½″ rectangles (U)
½ yard fusible stabilizer (e.g. Pellon Craft-Fuse)	MAIN LINING INTERFACING	(2) 7¼″ × 9½″ rectangles (V)
	ZIPPER PANEL INTERFACING	(2) 2″ x 13½″ strips (W)
	HANDLES INTERFACING	(2) 4″ x 12½″ strips (X)
	GUSSET LINING INTERFACING	(1) 3¾″ x 24½″ strip (Y)

ADDITIONAL SUPPLIES

- Adhesive basting spray • Binding clips • (1) 12″ nylon zipper • (1) 14″ zipper
- (17) 1″ hexagon paper pieces (see page 30 for the template)

CONSTRUCTION NOTE

When the term 'fuse' is listed in the instructions for any materials that are not fusible stabilizer, use basting spray to fuse the pieces together.

ASSEMBLING THE FRONT POCKET

1 Following the instructions on page 30, baste the A squares to the 1˝ paper hexagon pieces for a total of 17 hexagons. Referencing Figure 1, arrange the basted hexagons as shown. Sew the hexagons together in five vertical columns of three or four each and then hand sew the columns together. Remove the papers and trim to a 7½˝ × 5¼˝ rectangle.

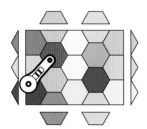

Figure 1

2 Following the manufacturer's instructions, apply basting spray to the wrong side of the assembled unit from Step 1. Center the B Batting rectangle on top and quilt as desired.

3 Sew H rectangles to the short edges of the quilted unit from Step 2 (Fig. 2). Smooth the wrong side of the H rectangles on the Batting using basting spray to adhere. Topstitch ⅛˝ away from the seams on the denim. Trim to 9½˝ × 5¼˝.

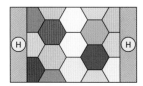

Figure 2

4 Apply a layer of basting spray to the wrong side of the I rectangle and layer the C Batting rectangle on top for the exterior top of the Front Pocket.

5 Trim the 12˝ zipper down to 9½˝ long. Fold one J rectangle in half so that the short ends meet. Fold each short end under by ¼˝ and press. Open up a J tab and sandwich one end of the zipper tape inside, between the folded ends. Being sure not to overlap the zipper stop. Topstitch ⅛˝ from the folded short ends to hold the zipper tab in place. Repeat with the other J rectangle and attach to the opposite end of the zipper tape. (Fig. 3)

Figure 3

6 Follow the directions for finishing the zipper pouch on page 31 through Step 2 using the O and P rectangles and the assembled units from Steps 3-5.

7 With adhesive basting spray, fuse a V Interfacing rectangle to the wrong side of a Q rectangle and a D Batting rectangle to the wrong side of another Q rectangle. Fuse V and D together. (Fig. 4)

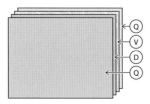

Figure 4

8 Place the Front Pocket on top of the layered stack from Step 7 with the Lining sides together to make the Front Panel. Baste in place with a zigzag stitch no more than ⅛" from edge. (Fig. 5)

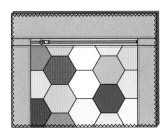
Figure 5

ASSEMBLING THE BACK PANEL

1 Fuse the V Interfacing to the wrong side of a Q Exterior rectangle and a D Batting rectangle to the K Lining. Then fuse the V and D pieces together to make the Back panel. (Fig. 6)

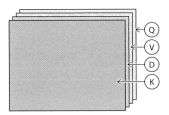
Figure 6

2 Fold the S rectangle in half with the WST, so the short ends meet. Press along the fold. Apply basting spray to both sides of the G Interfacing, open the S rectangle and position the G Interfacing inside. Refold the S rectangle and smooth the fabric over the Interfacing, adhering the layers together. Topstitch ⅛" from the fold.

Figure 7

3 Place the Pocket on the Lining side of the Back panel from Step 1, aligning the lower edge. Zigzag stitch ⅛" from the edge around the entire Back panel to secure the layers. (Fig. 8)

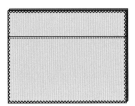
Figure 8

ASSEMBLING THE GUSSET

1 Make strap pieces from the U rectangles referencing the instructions on page 32. Fold each U piece in half so the short ends meet. Baste the short ends together.

2 Fuse the E Batting and L Exterior rectangles together to form two units. Fuse the wrong side of the R Lining rectangles and W Interfacing strips together to form two units. Follow the directions for finishing the zipper pouch on page 31 through Step 2 using the E and R strips and the zipper.

3 Topstitch ¼˝ from the zipper on either side, quilting the Exterior and Lining pieces together. Add additional parallel quilting lines if desired. Trim the panel to 13¼˝ × 3¾˝, ensuring the zipper is in the center of the panel. Center the raw edges of each U piece from Step 1 at either end of the zipper and sew in place ⅛˝ from the end.

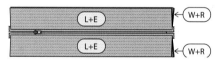

Figure 9

4 Fuse the wrong sides of M Exterior and F Batting rectangles together to create the Exterior Gusset and the wrong sides of the T Lining and Y Interfacing rectangles to create the Gusset Lining.

5 Stack in this order from bottom to top along one short end: Exterior Gusset (right side up), Zipper panel from Step 3 (right side down) and Gusset Lining (right side down). Stitch together along the left short end. Fold the gusset pieces away from the Zipper panel with the WST and topstitch ⅛˝ from the seam through all the layers. (Fig. 10)

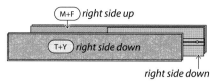

Figure 10

6 Repeat Step 5 on the opposite side of the Zipper panel with the other short ends of the gusset pieces. Flip them over or under the Zipper panel to get them in place correctly. Turn the Gusset Tube right side out and zigzag stitch around both sides of the Tube before turning it wrong side out again. (Fig. 11)

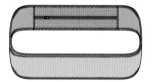

Figure 11

ASSEMBLING THE HANDLES

1 Fuse the N rectangles and Interfacing rectangles together and make two Handles by following the instructions on page 32.

2 Position the raw ends of the Handles in place along the upper edge of the exterior of the Front Pocket and Back panel. The outer edge of each Handle end should be 2½˝ away from each side. Baste in place to create the two Main panels. (Fig. 12)

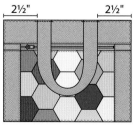

Figure 12

ATTACHING THE GUSSET

1 Use a disappearing ink marker to mark the center of both long sides of the Zipper panel and the center upper edge of both Main panels. Match a dot on the Zipper panel with one on the Front Main panel, keeping both RST. Pin or clip in place and sew along the edge stopping ¼" away from each corner, backstitching at both ends. (Fig. 13)

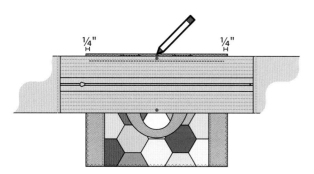

Figure 13

2 Fold the Gusset tube around the sides of the Front Main panel and hold in place with binding clips. Mitre the gusset at the corners just as you would when binding a corner of a quilt. Sew along the side edges, stopping ¼" before the corners and backstitching at the end of each side. (Fig. 14)

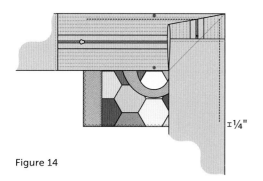

Figure 14

3 Finish attaching the Main panel to the Gusset with binding clips, smoothing the Gusset along the lower edge and keeping any excess fabric gathers at the corners. Sew the lower edges together, all the way to the corners, backstitching at each end. Unzip the zipper all the way so you will be able to turn the bag right side out later.

4 Repeat Steps 1-3 with the Back Main panel on the other side of the Gusset.

5 Finish the case by zigzag stitching twice around the exposed Lining seams on both Main panels. Turn right side out, pressing carefully to finish.

🎥 TOUR GUIDE

The trick to a neat finish on the inside seams is using a zigzag stitch on the edges of the gusset and main panels before you sew them together, keeping your stitches close together, and carefully trimming loose threads before and after you finish the seams.

Bandstand Mini Quilt

HISTORICAL MARKER

Our town's Memorial Park was just a block away from where I grew up, complete with modern bandstand and rusty old canon. Every summer, they held Sunday afternoon concerts in the park featuring a range of music styles from country to classical to swing, and the entire green would be packed with lawn chairs and quilts full of people there to listen. Patterned after the lattice that covered the top of that bandstand, this mini quilt takes me back to those dreamy moments just before dusk when music drifted across our neighborhood.

TOUR GUIDE

This project gave me the chance to play with value. White, gray, and black prints go from light to dark across the background, easily drawing the eye from one side to the other. I used solid colors for the crosses and a large scale dot print for the center squares, which I carefully fussy cut. Using a single print for the centers, even one with this much variety, holds everything together nicely.

FINISHED BLOCK SIZE: 4½˝ square
FINISHED QUILT SIZE: 22½˝ square

Pieced by Heidi Staples, quilted and bound by Jen Eskridge

ROTARY CLUB *Charm Square Friendly*

FABRIC	FOR	CUTTING
Fat quarter black large scale Dot Print	CENTER SQUARES	(25) 2″ squares (A)
5″ square each of 25 Solid fabrics in a rainbow of colors	CROSS SQUARES	(2) 2″ squares (B) (1) 2″ × 4″ rectangle (C)
5″ square of White Print		(2) 2″ × 4″ rectangles (D)
5″ square each of 2 Off-White Prints		(2) 2″ × 4″ rectangles from each print (E)
5″ square each of 3 Very Light Gray Prints		(2) 2″ × 4″ rectangles from each print (F)
5″ square each of 4 Light Gray Prints	BACKGROUND SQUARES	(2) 2″ × 4″ rectangles from each print (G)
5″ square each of 5 Gray Prints		(2) 2″ × 4″ rectangles from each print (H)
5″ square each of 4 Dark Gray Prints		(2) 2″ × 4″ rectangles from each print (I)
5″ square each of 6 Black Prints		(2) 2″ × 4″ rectangles from each print (J)
⅓ yard of Black and White Stripe Print	BINDING	(3) 2½″ × WOF strips

ADDITIONAL CUTTING AND SUPPLIES

FABRIC	CUTTING
Batting and Backing fabric	(1) 27″ square of each

ASSEMBLING THE BLOCKS

❶ First, sort the B and C pieces for each color into 25 separate stacks. Add an A square to each stack. On a flat surface, arrange the stacks into a 5 x 5 grid making diagonal color rows in red, pink, orange, yellow, green, aqua, blue, purple, and lavender as shown in the Assembly Diagram (see page 108). Add two D-J Background fabric rectangles to each stack creating a diagonal white-to-black Background gradient.

2 For each stack with the RST, sew the B squares to opposite sides of an A square. Sew the Background strips (D-J depending on block) to both long edges of the C rectangle. Press towards the solid colors on both units so that the seams nest correctly. Cut the second unit (C and Background strips) in half through all three strips so both halves measure 2˝ × 5˝. (Fig. 1)

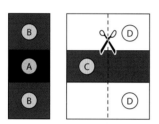

Figure 1

3 Sew the three units together to create a 9-Patch block (Fig. 2) pressing the seams in opposite directions for each row. Repeat with the remaining 24 stacks to create at total of 25 blocks.

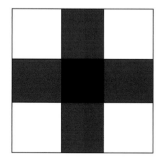

Figure 2

4 Recreate the 5 x 5 grid using the assembled blocks from Step 3. Check to make sure that your background fabrics create a pleasing gradient from white to black. Sew the blocks together in rows of five blocks each and press the seams in opposite directions so that they nest. Sew the rows together to finish the quilt top and press.

5 Quilt and bind as desired.

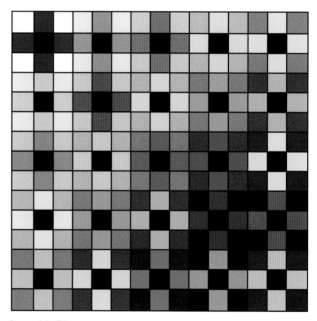

Assembly Diagram

Big Bear Cabin Quilt

FINISHED SIZE: 46″ square

Pieced by Heidi Staples, quilted and bound by Jen Eskridge

HISTORICAL MARKER

As I was sketching ideas on graph paper one day, I found myself marrying a log cabin block with a modified bear paw block and suddenly this quilt was born. Having spent the night in a log cabin style inn up at Big Bear Lake in the San Bernardino Mountains, I couldn't resist naming the pattern to match. You don't have to be sitting in front of a roaring fire with a cup of hot cocoa when you curl up under this quilt, but it sure doesn't hurt.

TOUR GUIDE

Alternating prints and solids for the rings and using a mix of prints for the half-square triangles, adds a nice variety to the pattern. I like to use a low volume print for one of the log cabin rings to give the quilt an unexpected accent.

 ROTARY CLUB

FABRIC	FOR	CUTTING
Scrap of Yellow Floral Print	CENTER BLOCK	(1) 2½" square (A)
2½" strips, each of Yellow Solid and Green Gingham Print	STARTING SQUARE OF LOG CABIN BLOCKS	(2) 2½" squares from each print (B)
2½" strips, each of low volume Floral and Green Print	SECOND RING OF LOG CABIN BLOCKS	(2) 2½" squares from each print (C) (2) 2½" × 4½" rectangles from each print (D)
2½" strips, each of Orange Solid and Aqua Plus Print	THIRD RING OF LOG CABIN BLOCKS	(2) 2½" × 4½" rectangles from each print (E) (2) 2½" × 6½" rectangles from each print (F)
2½" strips, each of Orange Leaf Print and Solid Aqua Print	FOURTH RING OF LOG CABIN BLOCKS	(2) 2½" × 6½" rectangles from each print (G) (2) 2½" × 8½" rectangles from each print (H)
2½" strips or a fat quarter each of Solid Pink and Blue Floral Print	FIFTH RING OF LOG CABIN BLOCKS	(2) 2½" × 8½" rectangles from each print (I) (2) 2½" × 10½" rectangles from each print (J)
2½" strips or a fat quarter each of Pink Geometric and Dark Navy Print	SIXTH RING OF LOG CABIN BLOCKS	(2) 2½" × 10½" rectangles from each print (K) (2) 2½" × 12½" rectangles from each print (L)
Scraps of 12 Brown Prints	HALF-SQUARE TRIANGLES	(1) 5" square from each print (M)
2 yards White Solid	BACKGROUND	(12) 5" squares (N) (4) 4½" squares (O) (4) 2½" × 16½" strips (P) (2) 6½" × 34½" strips (Q) (2) 6½" × 46½" strips (R)
½ yard Green Floral Print	BINDING	(5) 2½" × WOF strips

ADDITIONAL CUTTING AND SUPPLIES

FABRIC	CUTTING
Batting and Backing fabric	(1) 52" square of each

❶ Sort the B-L fabrics into two groups of cool colors and two groups of warm colors.

❷ Referencing the Log Cabin Assembly Diagram, sew the log cabin rings for one block, pressing each time a new fabric cut is added.

Rings 1-2: With the RST, sew a C square to the left edge of the B square. Sew a D strip to the upper edge of the unit.

Ring 3: Sew an E strip to the left edge of the unit. Sew an F strip to the upper edge of the unit.

Ring 4: Sew a G strip to the left edge of unit. Sew an H strip to the upper edge of the unit.

Ring 5: Sew an I strip to the left edge of the unit. Sew a J strip to the upper edge of the unit.

Ring 6: Sew a K strip to the left edge of the unit. Sew an L strip to the upper edge of the unit.

Log Cabin Assembly Diagram

③ Repeat Step 2 to create four Log Cabin Units.

④ Referencing the instructions on page 28 if necessary, use the M and N squares to make 24 half-square triangle units (HSTs), each 4½" square.

⑤ Referencing Figure 1, place 3 assembled HST units from Step 4 on each side of the outer ring of log cabin units with an O square at the corner. Sew the three units together on one side and then sew to the log cabin. Sew the remaining three HSTs plus the O square together and sew to the adjacent side to complete the quadrant. Repeat to create a total of four quadrants.

Figure 1

TOUR GUIDE

Try laying out all the pieces to see how the quilt will look as a whole before sewing the blocks together in Step 5 to get the right balance of colors and prints as you arrange the HST units.

⑥ Referencing the Assembly Diagram, arrange the four blocks from Step 5, the P strips and the A square on flat surface. Sew the pieces together in rows of three, press, and then sew rows together.

⑦ Sew the Q strips to the upper and lower edges of the assembled unit from Step 6. Press. Finally, sew the R strips to the left and right edges to complete the quilt top.

⑧ Quilt and bind as desired.

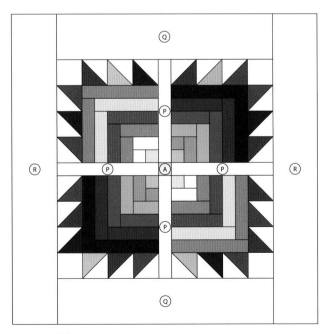

Assembly Diagram

LACY PARK QUILT

HISTORICAL MARKER

Occasionally on a Saturday afternoon when we were dating, James and I used to have picnics at Lacy Park in San Marino. We would bring a basket full of food and a book to read aloud to each other while we lay in the shade on a blanket and watched the clouds go by. It was heavenly. This quilt reminds me of those carefree days.

TOUR GUIDE

The key to this simple pattern is fussy cutting the flower centers and using two shades of the same color for the petals on each rose. The more prints you use, the lovelier this quilt will be.

FINISHED BLOCK SIZE: 10˝ square
FINISHED QUILT SIZE: 66˝ square

Pieced by Heidi Staples, quilted and bound by Jen Eskridge

① Separate the A-C prints into groups for each block. Add one D rectangle and four E rectangles to each group.

② For each block, sew a B and a C rectangle RST along their long edges. Press towards the C rectangle. Repeat with the C and D. Trim each pair into 4 sections 2½˝ wide. (Fig. 1)

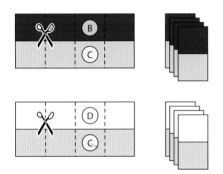

Figure 1

③ Referencing Figure 2, arrange the units into a 3 × 3 grid. Sew together in rows, press the seams in opposite directions so that they nest and then sew the rows together.

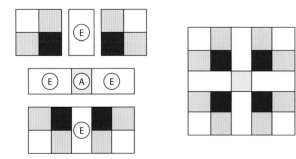

Figure 2

ROTARY CLUB

From scraps of 25 Focal Prints, cut:

(1) 2½˝ square from each print (A)

From a variety of 25 Prints in matching darker shades of A squares, cut:

(1) 2½˝ × 10˝ rectangle from each (B)

From a variety of 25 Prints in matching lighter shades of B rectangles, cut:

(1) 2½˝ × 10˝ rectangle from each (C)

From 1 yard of Background Fabric, cut:

(45) 2½˝ × 10˝ rectangles (D)

(100) 2½˝ × 4½˝ rectangles (E)

(4) 2½˝ × 58½˝ strips (F)

(2) 4½˝ × 58½˝ strips (G)

(2) 4½˝ × 66½˝ strips (H)

From ⅝ yard of a low volume Floral Print, cut:

(7) 2¼˝ × WOF strips (J)

From 4 yards of Batting and 108˝ wideback Backing fabric, cut:

(1) 72˝ square of each

④ Repeat Steps 2-3 to create a total of 25 blocks.

⑤ Referencing the Assembly Diagram, arrange the blocks into a 5 × 5 grid each. Add a remaining D rectangle between the blocks and sew together to form five rows. Sew an F strip between the rows and press. Sew the G strips to the top and bottom edges and press. Finally, sew the H strips to the right and left edges to finish the quilt top.

⑥ Quilt and bind as desired.

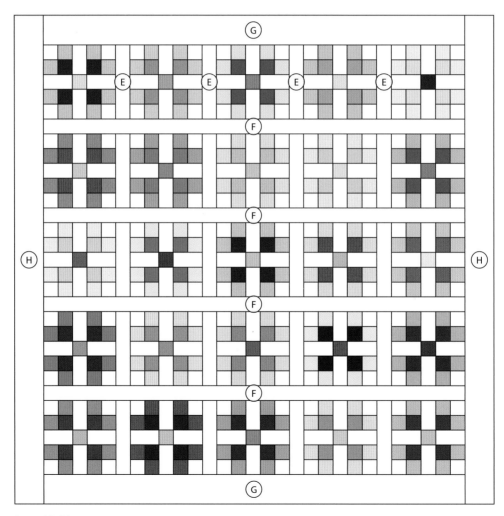

Assembly Diagram

CHAPTER FIVE

SHARE THE JOURNEY

There are so many ways to take this book on the road. Bring it on your next family vacation — along with your sewing machine, tools, and fabric, of course — to make some fun projects on the go. Pack it for an upcoming guild retreat or party to start some great group projects or spark ideas for swaps. Get together with friends to create a set of travel accessories for an upcoming girls' weekend or make a date with your kids to sew special pieces to celebrate the first day of school, an upcoming birthday party, or a family trip. Even if you're enjoying a sewing vacation at home, you'll find plenty of ideas in here to share mementos of your own creative journey by making gifts for the people you love.

TAGALONG PINCUSHION

- Make a sewing kit for a friend by tucking a pincushion, embroidery scissors, a small box of pins, and a thimble into a small basket. Add a few specially cut fabric pieces or a mini charm pack for an extra treat.

- Decorate a miniature tree with pincushions that feature fabric coordinating with whatever season is coming up. At the end of the get together, everyone can choose their favorite one off the tree to take home as a gift.

- Start off a sewing retreat by making this pincushion as a combination warm-up and get-to-know-you project. Have each person list a few of their favorite things (colors, themes, designers, etc.) on a card, exchange lists, and start sewing. Deliver your special gifts later in the day and make a new friend.

POSTCARD KIT

- Fill the kit with special photos and notes from friends and family for a loved one entering a new phase in life: a high school or college graduate, a friend who's moving to a new home, newlyweds, or new parents.

- Get your kids excited about an upcoming family adventure with one of these kits filled with stickers or coloring sheets that match the theme or destination of your trip. If you're making these beforehand to break the news as a surprise, have them guess the location based on the contents.

- Tuck love notes inside for a perfect Valentine's Day gift to a special someone.

- Make recipe kits! If you're on a sewing retreat with friends, have each person bring cards to share their favorite dishes for breakfast, lunch, dinner, and dessert (be sure to bring enough copies for everyone), and turn this into a special recipe card holder as a memory of your getaway.

 TOUR GUIDE

*Have time for just a short afternoon of sewing with friends? Decide on a project for your **sew-day** and share the work! Have one person cut all the background fabric, another cut all the lining **pieces**, and so on. Everyone goes home with a finish, and with everyone using the same fabric for certain **parts of the project**, you'll all have a special memory of your time together.*

ROAD TRIP PILLOW AND FIREWORKS PILLOW

- Surprise a new mom with a gift basket for late night feedings that includes a pillow, a good movie, and a few bags of microwave popcorn.

- Send a college freshman off to their new dorm room with a pillow in school colors.

- Make a set of pillows for a home or classroom reading nook.

SNAPSHOT NEEDLEBOOK AND HOBBY KIT

- Swap online or in person, pairing your favorite sewing title with a handmade needlebook and/or Hobby Kit.

- End a day at your sewing retreat with an evening of peaceful hand stitching. After Step 3 in the Needlebook or Step 2 in the Hobby Kit, gather on the porch, next to the pool, or down by the lake to add some embroidery or quilting to your patchwork before the sun goes down.

- Make a beginner kit packed with sewing essentials for a child who is learning to sew.

COFFEE SHOP COASTERS AND KITCHENETTE SET

- Welcome a new neighbor with a basket including a pair of mugs or milk glasses, a set of coasters and/or placemats and fresh cookies from your oven.

- Meeting up for a sew-day at a friend's house? Ask your hostess to select a favorite fabric collection or designer, color range, or theme so that each attendee can make up a coaster and a placemat as a thank-you. At the end of the day, she'll have a complete set!

BOARDWALK MINI TOTE, BEACHCOMBER BAG, AND PALM SPRINGS BAG

- Tuck a gift — any gift — inside one of these bags for perfect reusable wrapping.

- Sew bags with friends for a summer swap, being sure to add some vacation goodies like snacks, lip balm, sunscreen or a good book.

PENNY POUCH

- Make a manicure kit for a friend by filling a pouch with a few shades of polish, polish remover wipes, and a small set of manicure tools.

- Bring along one of these pouches for any networking conference. It's a great place to store business cards, stickers, pins and all the small ephemera so common at those events.

SOUVENIR CLUTCH AND CURIO POCKET

- Make a wedding day emergency kit for a friend who is getting married, including items like mints, safety pins, clear nail polish, tweezers, dental floss, bobby pins and of course, a mini sewing kit.

- Invite over some of your favorite tweens and/or teens to a school supply swap party and sew up a few of these. Fill them with pencils, erasers, a sharpener and other supplies.

BOOKMOBILE SLEEVE

- Slip a small sketchbook and set of colored pencils inside this sleeve to make a gift for the artist in your life.

- Host a book club with friends, gifting each member with their own sleeve.

- Make a set of sleeves for your child's classroom. The teacher can place a print book inside that can be loaned out to students.

SCOUT'S HONOR PENCIL CASE

- Make a set for your local scout troop or use them as party favors for a forest or camping themed birthday celebration.

- Personalize this by selecting 3 fabrics to fussy cut that will be inside jokes for your family about what happened on your latest vacation — a camping tent fabric to recall how hard it was to put up the tent in the dark or a number to represent how many state license plates you spotted along the way.

COLOR BOOK

- Make one of these as a gift for a toddler who's a new big brother or sister. Bring it along on your first visit to the newborn so that they can feel special too.

- Sew a set of color books for a preschool class, church nursery, or daycare center.

LAUNDROMAT COIN POUCH

- Instead of a tooth pillow, try using one of these as a tooth pouch.

- Fill with bandages, antibacterial cream, and alcohol swabs for an on-the-go first aid kit for your travels.

THE QUILTS

- These are wonderful collaborative projects to make on a retreat. Have each member make a block and you'll have a quilt top finished by the end. Hold a raffle for who gets to take it home or donate the finished quilt to a special local charity.

Coming Home

I always considered myself to be the nearest thing to a small-town girl that you could find in the Southern California suburbs.

I grew up in Sierra Madre, a city that filled less than 3 square miles in the foothills of the San Gabriel Mountains. Though it was just 18 miles northeast of Los Angeles, you couldn't find a stoplight anywhere in the city limits, and there was only one main street through town.

Our little house was built in the early 1900s with recycled lumber from a demolished barn, and I was the 4th generation of my mother's family to live in it. My sister and I rode our bikes on the sidewalk, gave impromptu concerts from the front porch, and spent hours playing in the yard until dark. When my mother wasn't working at the family business in town, she spent most of her free time with a sewing project in her hands: cross stitch, quilting, clothes for my sister and me. Seeing her creative work all around us in our home was such a comfort to me as a child, always reminding me that this was where I belonged, where I was loved. And as I watched my mother pour her heart into sewing for family and

friends, she taught me day by day that every task that passed through my hands could be a work of love.

Our family has grown a bit since those days, adding my husband and our three daughters to the mix. We've traded suburban life for a sprawling house in the Texas hill country that the seven of us — Dad, Mom, James, me, and the girls — all share together. Mom and I are still sewing from the heart, and now we're teaching my daughters to do the same. And home is still my favorite place in the world. So though everything has changed, nothing has changed . . . not really.

The patchwork projects in this book are inspired by the happy homes where I grew up and where I now live. It's been a joy for me to share them with you, and I hope that they'll bring beauty and delight to your everyday life. Because no matter where you're from or where you're going, you're creating memories for yourself and your loved ones, right now in the place you call home.

And maybe that's the greatest adventure of all.

IF I EVER GO LOOKING FOR
MY HEART'S DESIRE AGAIN,
I WON'T LOOK ANY FURTHER
THAN MY OWN BACK YARD.
BECAUSE IF IT ISN'T THERE,
I NEVER REALLY LOST IT TO
BEGIN WITH.

— L. FRANK BAUM

For the Road
TREATS TO MAKE THE TRIP EVEN MORE FUN

MAGIC BARS

These amazing bar cookies are like homemade candy bars. Bring a container full to share with friends at your next get together — and don't forget to save a few for snack time in your sewing room!

- 16-18 Honey Maid graham crackers, crushed into crumbs
- 1 cup butter
- ¾ c. chocolate chips
- ¾ c. white chocolate chips
- ¾ c. butterscotch chips
- ¾ c. Heath toffee pieces
- ¾ c. chopped macadamia nuts
- 1 cup sweetened flaked coconut
- 1 14 oz. can Eagle brand sweetened condensed milk

Heat oven to 350 degrees. Line a 9 x 13" cake pan with foil and coat with baking spray. Melt the butter and then stir in the graham cracker crumbs. Sprinkle them in the bottom of the pan, pressing them down to create a crust layer. Sprinkle all the remaining ingredients — except the last! — over the crust, finishing with the coconut. Pour the condensed milk evenly over the top. Bake until golden brown, about 25 minutes. Cool for 5-10 minutes, then carefully remove the bars in their foil lining from the pan to cool for another 2 hours. Slice into squares and serve.

TOMATO CUCUMBER SALAD   Serves 5-7

This summer salad is one of my favorite things to share at a family get together. I've made it for everything from a country barbecue to an elegant tea party, and it's always a big hit.

- 1 long seedless cucumber, peeled, quartered lengthwise, and chopped
- 1 12 oz. package of multicolored cherry tomatoes, halved
- ½ red onion, diced
- 1 8 oz. container of mozzarella pearls (drain liquid first)
- Salt & pepper
- Italian seasoning
- Red wine vinegar dressing (I use Brianna's Home Style Blush Wine Vinaigrette Dressing.)
- Balsamic vinegar reduction (I use Fini Reduction of Balsamic Vinegar of Modena.)

Add the first four ingredients to the bowl and mix well. Sprinkle on salt, pepper, and Italian seasoning to taste. Add the dressing (I use anywhere from ⅓-½ cup) and toss well. Drizzle the balsamic reduction on top to serve. (I always keep it on the table too, so that guests can add more if they like.)

Roadtrip Playlist

RETRO TUNES FOR HAPPY STITCHING

"AIN'T TOO PROUD TO BEG"

The Temptations

"ROUTE 66"

Chuck Berry

"PLEASE MR. POSTMAN"

The Marvelettes

"HELLO MARY LOU"

Ricky Nelson

"ORANGE COLORED SKY"

Nat King Cole

"KNOCK ON WOOD"

Eddie Floyd

"FUN, FUN, FUN"

The Beach Boys

"THE WEIGHT"

Aretha Franklin

"RUNAROUND SUE"

Dion

"LAZY RIVER"

Bobby Darin

"ON THE SUNNY SIDE OF THE STREET"

Peggy Lee

"SAVE THE LAST DANCE FOR ME"

The Drifters

Resources

ONLINE FABRIC SHOPS

Fat Quarter Shop
www.fatquartershop.com

Missouri Star Quilt Co.
www.missouriquiltco.com

Sew Me a Song
www.etsy.com/shop/sewmeasong

Sunny Day Supply
sunnydayfabric.com/

INFORMATION ON HOW TO SEW

Intentional Piecing
by Amy Friend for Lucky Spool Media

Lucky Spool Quilt Making Basics
luckyspool.com/collections/books/products/
lucky-spool-quilt-making-basics

The Quilt Block Cookbook
by Amy Gibson for Lucky Spool Media

School of Sewing: Learn It, Teach It, Sew Together
by Shea Henderson for Lucky Spool Media

SEWING PRODUCTS I USE

Aurifil Thread
www.aurifil.com

Clover Notions
www.clover-usa.com/en

Dritz Notions
www.dritz.com

Creative Grids Rulers
www.creativegridsusa.com

Gutermann Thread
www.gutermann.com/en

Olfa
www.olfa.com

Pellon Interfacing
www.pellonprojects.com

Riley Blake Designs
www.rileyblakedesigns.com

Robert Kaufman Fabrics
www.robertkaufman.com

Therm-O-Web Spray-n-Bond Adhesive Basting Spray
www.thermowebonline.com

Windham Fabrics
www.windhamfabrics.com

Acknowledgements

To Susanne for believing in this project and in me. It means more than I can say.

To Kristy, Nissa, Shea, Kari, Julie, Lisa, and Jen for turning my ideas into beautiful reality.

To Holly, Cindy and everyone from Riley Blake Designs. You have been incredibly generous and kind to me on this creative journey.

To wonderful friends — around the world and close to home — who bless my heart so much.

To David, Amy, Mike, Mary, Dave, Jenna, and all the cousins. I love you guys.

To Dad and Mom for their endless love and support. I couldn't love you more.

To my daughters, affectionately known as Bunny, Bear, and Mouse. You truly are the sunshine in my days. I love you, sweet girls.

To James … . for everything. I love you so much.

And to Jesus, my strength and joy. With all my heart, I thank you.

PENNY POUCH

Pattern B

Actual size

—— cut line

– – – stitch line

seam allowance